D. Caroline Coile, Ph.D.

Cavalier King Charles Spaniels

Everything about Purchasing, Care, Nutrition, Behavior, and Training

With 52 Color Photographs

Illustrations by Michele Earle-Bridges

BARRON'S

Acknowledgments

The information contained in this book comes from a variety of sources: breeders, original research, scientific articles, veterinary journals, and a library of dog books. But by far my most heartfelt gratitude must go to my most demanding teachers, who have taught me the skills of both home repair and dog repair, allowed ample testing opportunities for behavioral problem cures, and whetted my curiosity (and carpets) about everything canine for the past 20 years: Baha, Khyber, Tundra, Kara, Hypatia, Savannah, Sissy, Dixie, Bobby, Kitty, Jeepers, Bean-Boy, Junior, Khyzi, Wolfman, Stinky, Honey, and Luna

All inquiries should be addressed to:
Barron's Educational Series, Inc.
250 Wireless Boulevard
Hauppauge, NY 11788

ISBN-13: 978-0-7641-0227-1
ISBN-10: 0-7641-0227-3

Library of Congress Catalog Card 97-22429

Library of Congress Cataloging-in-Publication Data
Coile, D. Caroline.
    Cavalier King Charles spaniels / D. Caroline Coile.
       p.   cm. — (A complete pet owner's manual)
    Includes bibliographical references (p. 99) and index.
      ISBN 0-7641-0227-3
      1. Cavalier King Charles spaniel. I. Title. II. Series.
SF429.C36C65   1998
636.752′4—dc21   97-22429
                             CIP

Printed in China

20 19 18 17 16 15

About the Author

Caroline Coile is an award-winning author who has written articles about dogs for both scientific and lay publications. She holds a Ph.D. in the field of neuroscience and behavior, with special interests in canine sensory systems, genetics, and behavior. A sighthound owner since 1963, her own dogs have been nationally ranked in conformation, obedience, and field-trial competition.

Photo Credits

Toni Tucker: cover, page 40 top; Barbara Augello: inside front cover, pages 4, 17, 20, 24 top, 24 bottom, 28, 48, 81 top, 81 bottom, 84 top, 84 bottom, back cover; Bob Schwartz: pages 5, 8, 9, 12, 13 top, 13 bottom, 16 top, 16 bottom, 21, 25 top, 29, 36, 37, 40 bottom, 45, 53, 56, 60, 61, 64, 76 bottom, 77, 85, 88 top, 88 bottom, 89, 93, 96, 97, 100, inside back cover; Susan Green: page 25 bottom; Paulette Braun: pages 52, 57, 76 top; Norvia Behling: page 80; Janet York: page 92.

Important Notes

This pet owner's guide tells the reader how to buy and care for a Cavalier King Charles Spaniel. The author and the publisher consider it important to point out that the advice given in the book is meant primarily for normally developed puppies from a good breeder—that is, dogs of excellent physical health and good character.

Anyone who adopts a fully grown dog should be aware that the animal has already formed its basic impressions of human beings. The new owner should watch the animal carefully, including its behavior toward humans, and should meet the previous owner. If the dog comes from a shelter, it may be possible to get some information on the dog's background and peculiarities there. There are dogs that, as a result of bad experiences with humans, behave in an unnatural manner or may even bite. Only people that have experience with dogs should take in such animals.

Caution is further advised in the association of children with dogs, in meeting with other dogs, and in exercising the dog without a leash.

Even well-behaved and carefully supervised dogs sometimes do damage to someone else's property or cause accidents. It is therefore in the owner's interest to be adequately insured against such eventualities, and we strongly urge all dog owners to purchase a liability policy that covers their dog.

Contents

Preface

If the eyes are the window to the soul, the Cavalier King Charles Spaniel has the kindest soul in dogdom. To peer into the eyes of your Cavalier is to enjoy a vision of utter devotion and to fall completely under their spell. Those eyes have been working their magic on generations of some of the most powerful people in history. These kings may have ruled countries, but these spaniels ruled kings. Now Cavaliers are taking over families around the world.

Many popular breeds are totally unsuited for their roles as pets; the Cavalier is not one of them. Yet even this near perfect companion has some serious drawbacks and requires special care. This book is your guide to being as good to your Cavalier as it is to you.

The kindest eyes in all of dogdom.

The Cavalier is among the most adaptive of dogs when it comes to making itself at home, and is adept at turning any home into a castle.

King of Hearts

Among the many roles the dog has played throughout history, none has proved more valuable than that of companion. And few breeds have proved more companionable than the Cavalier King Charles Spaniel.

The Cavalier's uncanny companionship capabilities stem from its remote spaniel roots, dogs that were bred to hunt in partnership with their masters. Exactly when and how the hunting spaniel became the toy spaniel has been lost in antiquity. The breeding of small dogs was perfected in the ancient Orient, and the European toy spaniels were probably the result of breeding smaller spaniels to Oriental toy breeds such as the Japanese Chin and perhaps the Tibetan Spaniel—

The royal subject.

breeds that in turn could trace their own roots to the Maltese.

The Lap of Luxury

The lapdogs of Tudor Europe were every bit as vital to human comfort and health as were the glorified hunting dogs of the day. Lapdogs attracted fleas from their owners' bodies, thus lessening the human diseases and discomfort spread by these scourges. The dog's high body temperature also proved an asset in the lapdog's role as lap and foot warmer on cold wintry evenings at home or on long coach rides. Dogs were even welcomed into beds as foot warmers and heating pads. A warm dog placed on an aching joint or stomach could often help alleviate pain. In fact, lapdogs were sometimes credited with curing disease by extracting their owner's illness and taking it into their own bodies. While this is sheer myth, it's now accepted that dogs can improve the health of their owners just by cuddling and comforting. And one thing was as accepted in days of old as in modern times: these "comforter spaniels" did more than warm laps—they warmed hearts.

Several lapdog types vied for preeminence, but the toy spaniels had the advantage of appealing to every member of the family. The men of the manor might coax the little spaniels out of their ladies' laps for a foray in the field to hunt small game, such as rabbits or woodcock. The children found willing playmates in the little dogs. And the esthetic appeal of these dogs was evident to all. The little dogs thus served their people as hunters, companions, foot warmers, flea catchers, adornments, jesters, and confidants. Many breeds have tried to live up to such duties, but few as successfully as the little comforter spaniels.

The Dog Who Would Be King

The comforter spaniels wasted no time in weaving their way into every facet of their people's lives. These dogs became inseparable companions to the nobility, as evidenced by their inclusion in so many royal portraits. Few breeds have had their history documented in such royal fashion, painted by the most esteemed artists of their time. Whether cavorting underfoot, sitting majestically alongside, or lying comfortingly in a lap, the dogs of these fifteenth-century paintings look uncannily like the Cavaliers of today.

The comforter spaniels were a favorite of royalty throughout Europe. Mary Queen of Scots spent her youth in France, and was probably introduced to the spaniels there. She in turn has been credited with introducing the little dogs to Scotland and England. When, in 1587, she was led to the gallows, her faithful black and white toy spaniel refused to leave her side. It was later removed from beneath her skirts after her beheading.

England quickly became the adopted homeland for the toy spaniels, in great part because of the dedication of King Charles I. But like that of their royal owners, the fates of the royal spaniels were forever intertwined with their tumultuous times. On the same day that King Charles I was executed at the demand of Oliver Cromwell, Cromwell's men took the king's constant companion spaniel, Rogue, to publicly exhibit as a trophy.

By far the most credit for the unrivaled success of the toy spaniel can be attributed to King Charles II, who regained his father's throne and ruled England from 1660 to 1685. King

The Cavalier King Charles Spaniel (rear) compared to the English Toy Spaniel.

Charles was an unabashed aficionado of the little dogs, always having several in his company. In fact, the king was so preoccupied with his dogs that he was sometimes accused of ignoring concerns of the kingdom. One royal edict he did find time to make was that no toy spaniel could ever be denied entrance into any public building, including Parliament. It was not unusual for a dam with a litter of pups to be found in the king's bedchambers, and a dozen of his devoted spaniels comforted him on his deathbed. So much did the little dogs come to be identified with the king that they eventually came to be called "King Charles Spaniels."

After his death, King Charles's brother, James II, took over as both king and patron of the King Charles Spaniel. His reign lasted only a few years before he was exiled to France and William III took his place as king, but not as King Charles Spaniel advocate. The new ruler favored Pugs, and so the Pug usurped the toy spaniel as official royal dog.

But the Pug could not completely take over as the dog of the nobility. Through his association with King James, the Duke of Marlborough had

Selective breeding has restored the modern Cavalier to its King Charles time look.

King Charles Spaniels rivaled the Pug as the perennial favorite of aristocracy throughout the centuries. Queen Victoria was known for her affection for dogs of many breeds, but her particular favorite was a tricolor toy spaniel named Dash. Upon his death, his epitaph read "His attachment was without selfishness, his playfulness without malice, his fidelity without deceit."

Despite competition from the Pug, the King Charles Spaniel continued to grace the homes and cavort in the gardens of the wealthier families just as they had done for generations. But although they still displayed the typical gay, fearless, and loving temperaments that had so long endeared them to their families, their appearance was slowly changing.

Winners by a Nose

During King Charles's time, the toy spaniels had fairly long muzzles, flat skulls, and high-set ears, but by the late nineteenth century dogs with shorter muzzles, domed skulls, and low-set ears were the preferred and prevalent type. Around this same time dog showing was emerging as a pastime of the wealthy, and judging guidelines, or breed standards, were drawn up describing the ideal for each breed. The standard for the King Charles Spaniel required a domed skull and pushed-in nose. Those dogs not meeting these criteria did not win in the show ring, and thus were not sought as breeding stock. By the early twentieth century, few dogs remained that resembled the dog so popular in earlier times.

The king's spaniel was in peril, and it took a gallant knight to rescue it. That gallant knight was a wealthy American named Roswell Eldridge, who had become enthralled by the pointy-nosed spaniels pictured in the old royal paintings. So enamored was

become completely infatuated with the little spaniels. The duke bred mostly red and white King Charles Spaniels, which became known as Marlborough or Blenheim (pronounced "blennim") Spaniels. Supposedly, while the duke was away fighting in the battle of Blenheim, his wife was at home worrying about her husband and soothing a whelping bitch. The distraught duchess comforted both herself and the prospective mother by repeatedly pressing the bitch's forehead with her thumb. When news came that the battle had been won, the puppies were born, and all bore a red "thumbmark" in the middle of their forehead, said to have resulted from pressing the dam's forehead! Of course, such markings are due to genes, but at the time it was a popular explanation. The name Blenheim was applied to the red and white dogs with the characteristic "Blenheim spot." Generations of Dukes of Marlborough continued to breed their Blenheim strain until the early 1900s.

he that he traveled to England in 1926 to obtain a breeding pair for himself, but was sorely disappointed to find not a single such dog at any show. Mr. Eldridge then astounded the dog world by offering a dog show class prize of 25 pounds ($125) each for best male and female "Blenheim Spaniels of the Old Type, as shown in pictures of Charles II's time, long face, no stop, flat skull, not inclined to be domed, with spot in the center of skull." Most breeders who had been striving to produce only round-headed dogs were appalled, but nonetheless several entered their "worst" (that is, longest-nosed) in the competition, and a few deliberately bred these dogs together. Roswell Eldridge died without ever finding the dog of his dreams, but could scarcely have imagined the course of events his challenge would elicit. The seed he sowed fired the imagination of several breeders, who embraced the vision of recreating the original royal spaniels. In 1928 the first Cavalier club was formed, the first standard (modeled after a dog named Ann's Son) was written, and the English Kennel Club recognized the new type as King Charles Spaniels, Cavalier type. The name Cavalier was in homage to the political group that restored Charles II to the throne after the death of Oliver Cromwell. The name seems particularly fitting to denote these dogs who were now being restored to their place of royalty.

Within a few years long-nosed Cavaliers were gracing the show rings as well as fine homes, although their numbers were still limited. With the Second World War came a devastating setback, as most of the breeding stock had to be destroyed because of hardship. Eventually, six dogs came to be the foundation from whom all modern Cavaliers descend. Their numbers and quality gradually increased, and the Cavalier was granted status in 1945 as a separate breed, the Cavalier King Charles Spaniel.

The Cavalier versus the English Toy Spaniel

The Cavalier King Charles Spaniel and the English Toy Spaniel are constantly confused with one another. To further complicate matters, in England the English Toy Spaniel is known as the King Charles Spaniel and in the United States, one of its color varieties is known as King Charles. The two breeds resemble one another and, until the last hundred years, shared the same history and came from the same stock. The breeds come in the same four colors, but we call two of the colors by different names. The English Toy Spaniel is divided into two color varieties, the solid body colors (ruby and King Charles) and the broken colors (Blenheim and Prince Charles). The Cavalier does not separate the breed into varieties. See comparisons table on page 10.

Haute Dogs

Despite acceptance by the Kennel Club, popularity of the Cavalier rose slowly—that is, until 1973. One of the largest and most prestigious dog shows in the world is England's Crufts Dog Show. In 1973 a Cavalier named Alansmere Aquarius bested thousands

The finest of dogs for the finest of homes.

	Cavalier	English Toy (King Charles)
weight	13–18 pounds (6–8 kg)	9–12 pounds (4–5.5 kg)
muzzle length	medium	short
skull	flat	domed
ear set	high	low
tail	undocked or docked long	docked short
colors		
red, white	Blenheim	Blenheim
black, tan, white	tricolor	Prince Charles
red	ruby	ruby
black, tan	black and tan	King Charles

of other dogs to emerge as the Best in Show at Crufts, thrusting the Cavalier into the limelight. No longer was the Cavalier the closely guarded secret of the wealthy; the little dogs with the teddy bear eyes were suddenly the darling of everybody. This was the break the breed had been waiting for, but it was not without its downside. Now there was a ready market prepared to pay top dollar for an irresistible puppy. Unfortunately, there were unscrupulous breeders ready to cash in, producing as many puppies as possible without concern for quality. Those pups in turn were bred by their naive owners, who never realized their dogs were not up to snuff. As supply exceeded demand, prices dropped, and those who were never really in love with the breed except for its money-making potential deserted them for the next fad breed. Today the Cavalier is the most popular toy breed in England; in fact, it is one of the most popular of all breeds there. Most breeds that have achieved such popularity are rife with hereditary problems due to uneducated or uncaring breeders. The Cavalier has sidestepped this destiny to some degree, but still has suffered from popularity.

The Controversy on the Continent

Meanwhile, the situation was very different in the United States. For Americans, lacking the constant reminders of royal heritage and oblivious to the existence (yet alone outcome) of the Crufts Dog Show and its supreme victor, the Cavalier remained an anonymous face. Yet early paintings suggest that Cavaliers had made their way to the New World in Colonial times, and there was steady documented importation to America from England from 1946 on. A group of enthusiasts formed the Cavalier King Charles Spaniel Club, USA (CKCSC, USA) in 1954. The club sought recognition for the breed from the American Kennel Club (AKC), and in 1961 the AKC accepted the Cavalier into its miscellaneous class, a sort of staging area for new breeds. Still, too few Cavaliers existed in America to warrant official breed status, so the CKCSC, USA held its own shows and awarded its own championships while awaiting an increase in the breed population. The breed grew so much that the club's specialty shows attracted entries of as many as 300 Cavaliers. Official AKC recognition seemed imminent, and the invitation finally came in 1993.

Few clubs can claim the success that the CKCSC, USA has achieved, both in terms of numbers of members and service to the breed. The club maintains complete records of all Cavalier pedigrees, litters, and registered dogs. Members must abide by a strict code of ethics, which governs (among other topics) the age and number of times a dog can be bred, and the criteria for receiving full recognition. AKC recognition would mean giving the duties of registration to the AKC, thus giving up the club's quality control guidelines. These guidelines had helped keep the breed out of the hands of unscrupulous breeders, who would have found it nearly impossible to register their stock, and thus would have had difficulty selling inferior puppies. In addition, without the catch phrase "AKC registered," the puppy market would not be strong, further discouraging careless or profit-motivated breeding. Many members of the CKCSC, USA feared that AKC recognition would propel the Cavalier into the popular limelight and result in a repeat of the situation that had ultimately hurt the breed in England.

Thus, when the invitation came, it was not met with universal glee. The CKCSC, USA polled its members, who voted overwhelmingly (1,237 to 117) against accepting the AKC's invitation. While all members wanted the best for their beloved breed, they disagreed about the best way to serve it. The dissenting voters feared that if AKC did not recognize the CKCSC, USA as the parent club for the breed, they might recognize a parent club formed of less experienced and less devoted fanciers. In self-defense they formed the American Cavalier King Charles Spaniel Club (ACKCSC) and offered themselves as the official parent club to AKC. The AKC then officially welcomed the Cavalier into its toy group on January 1, 1996.

The Cavalier was an instant success in the show ring, quickly winning the admiration of judges and the hearts of spectators. Forewarned by the fate of their cousins in England, Cavalier fanciers are careful to promote their breed cautiously and place them only with the greatest care lest they fall into unscrupulous hands. Anyone trying to obtain a Cavalier from an ethical breeder must be prepared to be given the third degree.

The Cavalier remains a fairly expensive dog and is still relatively uncommon in America. It continues to appeal to the upper crust of society throughout Europe and America. But more and more, the little spaniel with the royal cape and pauper eyes can be found transforming humble homes into Cavalier castles and any lap into the lap of luxury.

To Cav or Cav Not...

What would your ideal companion dog be like? Would it eagerly join you on a jaunt afield, bounding ahead but taking care never to wander too far? Would it be just as content to spend a rainy day snuggling in your arms as you both loll in front of a roaring fire? Would it follow your directions with tail awag, ever eager for your next idea? Would it be a gentle and trustworthy special friend for a child, yet sound the alarm to a stranger's presence? Then meet the Cavalier King Charles Spaniel.

A Cavalier Attitude

How can one breed be so nearly the perfect canine companion? Because it was bred to be. The Cav's hunting spaniel heritage infused it with a basic

A fortuitous blend of obedience and playfulness.

sense of adventure and outdoor hardiness. The Cavalier King Charles Spaniel is at heart a sporting dog, and is delighted at the chance to get back to its roots, never missing an opportunity to launch itself into a lake or beat the bushes for birds.

Though the Cavalier does have a wild side, it is tamed by an even stronger desire to please its human partner. Because a working spaniel must heed the hunter's directions, those early spaniels that ran amok in the field were not used to create the next generation of hunters, with the result that today's Cavalier has behind it generation after generation of dogs that were eager to comply with their masters' wishes.

No doubt the Cavalier's easy trainability enabled it to worm its way into its master's—and mistress's—hearts and hearths. Once there, those dogs that particularly enjoyed staying by the side or in the lap of their owners were especially prized. Dogs that were always underfoot had to be trustworthy with children, and, of course, no one could have just one Cavalier, so the little spaniels had to also get along with each other. Selection for these traits—obedience, sociability, and tractability—combined with the spaniel's innate joie de vivre and quest for adventure—created a dog that was the ideal companion. These very traits are the hallmark of today's Cavaliers.

Still, there are other breeds that are both obedient and fun-loving. What makes the Cavalier King Charles Spaniel so special?

Cavalier Considerations

Trainability: There are breeds that are faster to learn and faster to respond than the Cavalier. In fact, a popular book ranks the Cavalier near the middle (72 out of 133) of breeds compared for obedience and working intelligence. But you don't necessarily want your dog to rank at the top of this list. The Cavalier is too calm and low key to be a hop-to-it obedience whiz dog. It was bred to be a house companion and, as such, doesn't have the excessive activity and energy level required to excel in working obedience tests.

Size: Called the king-sized toy, the Cavalier is the largest breed in the toy group, and in some ways combines the best of both small- and medium-size dogs. Small dogs are more economical to feed, house, and even take traveling. Small enough to tuck under your arm, yet large enough to trot alongside, the Cav's size makes it an ideal companion whether on a trip to town or cross-country. At home, the Cavalier is just the right size for cuddling, yet large enough to jump on and off your sofa or bed (if you let it) by itself, something that can be difficult or dangerous for tiny dogs.

Exercise: The Cavalier's size makes it at home in either an apartment or house, but its sporting heritage does make it necessary for it to get outdoors and run off excess energy at least once a day. Still, the Cavalier is too small to be a jogging companion for a marathon runner. And despite the Cav's friendly nature, owners must be cautioned that not all dogs are so friendly in turn, and the Cavalier is virtually defenseless against bigger dogs. As such, it should never be taken to run off-lead in areas where large dogs are also running free. In fact, the Cavalier should never be let off-lead except in the safest of places, because the

The Cavalier is also content to take life easy.

Cavalier is too easily tempted by the smallest diversion. Even a fluttering butterfly can lure a cavorting Cavalier into the path of traffic. In too many instances, curiosity killed the Cav.

Children: Rough children, too, can pose a danger to a small dog,

The amiable Cavalier gets along well with children and other dogs.

13

Cavaliers have a tendency to throw caution to the wind when the chance for a game arises. They can become so engrossed in what they are doing that they fail to realize that they may be in danger.

especially a tolerant one. The Cavalier is extremely gentle, but every dog has its limit. Your Cav should not be pushed to the point of defending itself; it is the parent's duty to oversee any child playing with a Cav, because the Cavalier is too small for rough-and-tumble play or careless handling.

Protection: What a joke! The Cavalier's bark is indeed worse than its bite. It will welcome burglars with great gusto, with wagging tail and soaring spirit. Although some may find a barking Cavalier to be intimidating, in truth the Cavalier is not a particularly effective protection dog.

Grooming: The Cavalier is blessed with the best of all worlds when it comes to its eye-catching coat. It is long enough to be luxuriously soft when cuddling, yet not so thick that constant grooming is required. As an added bonus, the Cav's coat comes in a variety of colors.

Grooming the Cavalier will require a couple of short weekly sessions, con-sisting of brushing or combing the longer hair while paying special attention to areas that tend to mat. Bathing is only rarely needed. The Cavalier sheds neither more nor less than most other breeds.

Royal Colors

The Cavalier comes in two different colors (black and tan, or red), and two different patterns (solid, or broken with white) for a total of four different color varieties:

Ruby: a solid rich tan or red, also described as chestnut.

Black and tan: distributed as the black and tan coloration of the Doberman pinscher.

Blenheim: rich tan or red broken up by large white areas. The color extends over both eyes and ears, with a large blaze covering the muzzle and extending between the eyes. A small colored spot in the middle of the blaze near the back of the skull is commonly seen and desirable.

Tricolor: the black and tan pattern broken up by white in the same basic pattern as that seen in the Blenheim.

Each color has its own appeal, although the Blenheim is undeniably the most popular. Many owners of Cavaliers eventually find that they must have one of each!

Cavalier Caveats

Does the Cavalier sound too good to be true? Unfortunately there is a serious downside to Cavalier ownership. Although generally a healthy and long-lived breed, looming in the Cav's genetic background is the haunting problem of hereditary defects; the most heartbreaking those involving the heart.

Cardiac problems: About 50 percent of all Cavaliers over the age of four have a heart murmur resulting from deterioration of the mitral valve. Some affected dogs can still live to ripe old ages, even 15 or 16 years, but, sadly, the heart problem cuts short the lives of far too many.

Many breeders of Cavaliers have encountered the devastating effects of this heart disease and are determined to eradicate it from the breed. Dedicated breeders never breed a Cavalier unless it has first been cleared by a veterinary cardiologist. Breeding stock should be checked every two years, starting at the age of two.

Note that a mitral valve murmur should not be confused with an innocent flow murmur, a common but harmless murmur found in many young dogs. This is why examination by a certified veterinary cardiologist is preferable to one by a general veterinarian. Mitral valve disease is described in greater detail on page 68.

Orthopedic problems: The Cavalier is in the unfortunate position of being one of the few breeds to be prone to both hip dysplasia (the bane of many large breeds) and patellar luxation (the bane of many small breeds).

In hip dysplasia, the ball and socket of the hip joint is poorly fit. Most often, the socket (the acetabulum of the pelvis) is too shallow, allowing the ball (head of the femur bone) to slip, gradually wearing away at both bony surfaces. Hip dysplasia is nearly impossible to diagnose by simply looking at a dog, although a stilted gait, difficulty in jumping or in rising, or a swaying movement in the rear can be suggestive of a hip problem. A diagnosis requires radiographic evaluation. A general veterinarian can take the X ray, which is then submitted to the Orthopedic Foundation for Animals (OFA) for evaluation. A more recent diagnostic technique, the "PennHIP," can diagnose and quantify the severity of a hip problem in puppies as young

as 16 weeks of age, but a PennHIP-certified veterinarian must perform the evaluation.

Hip dysplasia is thought to be the result of a combination of several genes, further modified by environmental factors. It is possible for a dysplastic dog to be born of normal parents and for a normal dog to be born of dysplastic parents, but, in general, like begets like. Choose a dog from stock that has been certified clear by either OFA or PennHIP. If your puppy is at least 16 weeks of age, you might ask that your purchase be contingent upon a PennHIP evaluation.

In patellar luxation, the patella (kneecap) often pops out of place. In normal dogs the patella rides in a groove along the front of the femur, but in some dogs the groove is too shallow. When the dog runs or jumps, or, in some cases, merely trots, the patella dislocates and the dog is unable to bend its leg. Dogs will often exhibit a characteristic hop in which one of the hind legs is carried up and forward for a step or two at a time. Viewed from the rear, the leg will appear to bow in or out around the area of the stifle (knee).

Luxating patellas can often be diagnosed before one year of age, and they can be surgically corrected by deepening the groove. The sooner this surgery is performed, the better the prognosis for a pain-free gait throughout the dog's life. However, this condition has a hereditary basis and affected dogs should not be bred. Breeding stock should be checked clear prior to breeding, and rechecked regularly, because not all cases can be diagnosed at an early age.

Ocular problems: Many Cavaliers have teary eyes, usually as a result of entropion. In this condition the eyelid folds abnormally, so that the lid and lashes turn in on the eye and irritate it.

The best pups come from the best families.

even eventually cause blindness. Most cases are far from being so severe, however. Entropion seems to have a hereditary basis, and affected dogs should not be bred.

Like many breeds, Cavaliers can suffer from cataracts, an opacity of the lens. Cataracts that appear at an early age are believed to be hereditary. An affected lens can be removed, but such dogs should not be bred.

Retinal dysplasia is an abnormal development of some of the visual cells of the retina, ultimately leading to blindness. There is no cure, but the condition can be discovered by a veterinarian or veterinary ophthalmologist at only a few weeks of age. This means that a buyer can have a pup checked before falling in love with it, only to see it later succumb to a life in the dark. Some concerned breeders will have their entire litters checked before offering them for sale, and any breeder should agree to having a pup tested before you buy it.

In Cavaliers, the lower lid is most often the culprit. Entropion can be extremely irritating, but can be corrected surgically. Left untreated, it can lead to corneal ulceration, which could

Before You Buy

Don't rush to find a Cavalier without pausing to remember why you want a dog, and especially a Cavalier, in the first place. Chances are you want a healthy, fun-loving, amiable little dog that can play tirelessly and look beautiful. Thus, you want to find a dog with the four cornerstones of Cavalier perfection: good health, temperament, type, and soundness.

Health: Cavaliers are generally a healthy and hardy breed, commonly reaching 11 years of age, and sometimes 15 or 16 years. The chances of sharing a long life with your Cavalier will be greatly increased if you carefully screen your source to ensure that your potential pup is as free as possible of hereditary problems.

When buying a Cavalier pup, you should be even more careful than when buying most other breeds of dogs. Do not get your Cavalier from

The royal colors: Blenheim, black and tan, ruby, and tricolor.

someone who is oblivious to the breed's possible health problems, especially cardiac problems. In the best scenario, your pup's parents would have the following clear certifications:
• free of mitral valve murmur from a veterinary cardiologist within the past two years
• free of hip dysplasia
• free of patellar luxation within the past two years
• free of ocular problems from the Canine Eye Registry Foundation within the past two years

Note: Insist upon seeing any such certification firsthand.

If the pup's background checks out, then examine the puppy itself.
• Your pup should have its first vaccinations and dewormings.
• It should be clean, with no missing hair, crusted or reddened skin, or signs of parasites. Eyes, ears, and nose should be free of discharge.
• The pup should not be coughing, sneezing, or vomiting.
• Gums should be pink; pale gums may indicate anemia.
• Examine the eyelids to ensure that the lids or lashes don't roll into the eye. Pay special attention to the bottom lids.
• The area around the anus should have no indication of redness or irritation.
• The pup should not be thin or pot-bellied.
• If you pick up a fold of skin and release it, it should "pop" back into place. If it stays tented up, then it could indicate dehydration and suggest repeated vomiting or diarrhea.
• Male pups should have two testicles in the scrotum.

Temperament: A healthy dog should be a top priority for any breeder, and it should be a top priority for any buyer. But the healthiest of dogs is no bargain if it doesn't have a

It may be impossible to choose between these two healthy looking youngsters.

healthy outlook on life, so you will also want to ask your source several more questions:
• Can you meet the dam, and perhaps the sire of the puppy? Their personality is your best indicator of your future pup's.
• Are there any dogs with obedience titles within the last two generations? Such titles indicate not only obedient ancestors, but breeders who care about temperament.
• Was the puppy raised in a home environment? Pups raised with minimal human contact may have some personality problems.

Cavalier pups should be outgoing and active. Avoid any that show signs of fearfulness or aggressiveness. If they are apathetic or sleepy, it could be that they have just eaten, but it could also be a sign of sickness.

1. Muzzle
2. Stop
3. Skull
4. Neckline
5. Withers
6. Shoulder
7. Back
8. Loin
9. Croup
10. Tail
11. Forechest
12. Upper arm
13. Pastern
14. Elbow
15. Ribcage
16. Knee
17. Hock
18. Thigh

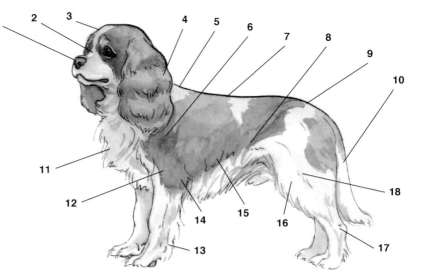

External anatomy of the Cavalier King Charles Spaniel.

Type: If your prospective puppy meets both your health and temperament criteria, then move on to consider the aspect of type. Type refers to those traits that distinguish one breed from another. After all, you want your Cavalier King Charles Spaniel to look like a Cavalier. Again, you will want to ask your source several questions:
· Can you see pictures of the sire and dam, or see them "in person"? Their appearance is the best clue to the future appearance of their offspring.
· Can you see the pedigree of the sire and dam?
· Can you see the litter registration for the puppy? Never get a puppy without proof of registration.
· Are there any conformation champions within the first two generations of the pedigree?
To fully understand type, you need to study the standard, the official blueprint for the breed. Even if you don't demand

perfection, some traits are essential in order for your Cavalier to be recognized as a Cavalier King Charles Spaniel. The hallmark of the Cavalier is its expression, especially its large, round, dark eyes, peering straight ahead into your eyes with a look of pure innocence. The high-set ears give the top of the head a somewhat flat appearance. The nose in the adult is about 1½ inches (3.8 cm) long and is neither pointed nor pug. The hair is soft, silky, and as straight as possible, with vibrant colors in one of the four accepted patterns. Adult size is from 13 to 18 pounds (6–8 kg), and height from 12 to 13 inches (31–33 cm).

Soundness: The ideal Cavalier will have the best of health, temperament, and type, and on top of that, should be sound. Soundness refers to the ability to move efficiently so that your Cav can run and play tirelessly. Avoid dogs from parents whose feet all point in different directions, or that are extremely cowhocked (with heels pointing inward), or have any difficulty in getting around. Avoid a limping puppy (if everything else about the pup is to your liking, ask to see it in another few days). Soundness is a trait more vital to the show dog than to the pet, but should nonetheless never be ignored.

AKC Standards

General Appearance—The Cavalier King Charles Spaniel is an active, graceful, well-balanced toy spaniel, very gay and free in action; fearless and sporting in character, yet at the same time gentle and affectionate. It is this typical gay temperament, combined with true elegance and royal appearance, which are of paramount importance to the breed. Natural appearance with no trimming, sculpting, or artificial alteration is essential to breed type.

Size, Proportion, Substance—Size—Height 12 to 13 inches [31–33 cm] at the withers; weight proportionate to height, between 13 and 18 lbs. [6–8 kg]. A small, well-balanced dog within these weights is desirable, but these are ideal heights and weights and slight variations are permissible. Proportion—The body approaches squareness, yet if measured from point of shoulder to point of buttock, is slightly longer than the height at the withers. The height from the withers to the elbow is approximately equal to the height from the elbow to the ground. Substance—Bone moderate in proportion to size. Weedy and coarse specimens are to be equally penalized.

Head—Proportionate to size of dog, appearing neither too large nor too small for the body. Expression—The sweet, gentle, melting expression is an important breed characteristic. Eyes—Large, round, but not prominent and set well apart; color a warm, very dark brown; giving a lustrous, limpid look. Rims dark. There should be cushioning under the eyes, which contributes to the soft expression. Faults—Small, almond-shaped, prominent, or light eyes; white surrounding ring. Ears—Set high, but not close, on top of the head. Leather long with plenty of feathering and wide enough so that when the dog is alert, the ears fan slightly forward to frame the face. Skull—Slightly rounded, but without dome or peak; it should appear flat because of the high placement of the ears. Stop is moderate, neither filled nor deep. Muzzle—Full muzzle slightly tapered. Length from base of stop to tip of nose about 1½ inches [3.8 cm]. Face well filled below eyes. Any tendency toward snippiness undesirable. Nose pigment uniformly black without flesh marks and nostril well developed. Lips well developed but not pendulous, giving a clean finish. Faults—Sharp or pointed muzzles. Bite—A perfect, regular, and complete scissors bite is preferred, i.e., the upper teeth closely overlapping the lower teeth and set square into the jaws. Faults—Undershot bite, weak or crooked teeth, crooked jaws.

Neck, Topline, Body—Neck—Fairly long, without throatiness, well enough muscled to form a slight arch at the crest. Set smoothly into nicely sloping shoulders to give an elegant look. Topline—Level both when moving and standing. Body—Short-coupled with ribs well sprung but not barreled. Chest moderately deep, extending to elbows, allowing ample heart room. Slightly less body at the flank than at the last rib, but with no tucked-up appearance. Tail—Well set on, carried happily but never much above the level of the back, and in constant characteristic motion when the dog is in action. Docking is optional. If docked, no more than one third to be removed.

"The sweet, gentle, melting expression is an important breed characteristic."
—AKC standard

Forequarters—Shoulders well laid back. Forelegs straight and well under the dog with elbows close to the sides. Pasterns strong and feet compact with well-cushioned pads. Dewclaws may be removed.

Hindquarters—The hindquarters construction should come down from a good broad pelvis, moderately muscled; stifles well turned and hocks well let down. The hindlegs when viewed from the rear should parallel each other from hock to heel. Faults—Cow or sickle hocks.

Coat—Of moderate length, silky, free from curl. Slight wave permissible. Feathering on ears, chest, legs and tail should be long, and the feathering on the feet is a feature of the breed. No trimming of the dog is permitted. Specimens where the coat has been altered by trimming, clipping, or by artificial means shall be so severely penalized as to be effectively eliminated from competition. Hair growing between the pads on the underside of the feet may be trimmed.

Color—Blenheim—Rich chestnut markings well broken up on a clear, pearly white ground. The ears must be chestnut and the color evenly spaced on the head and surrounding both eyes, with a white blaze between the eyes and ears, in the center of which may be the lozenge or "Blenheim spot." The lozenge is a unique and desirable, though not essential, characteristic of the Blenheim. Tricolor—

Jet black markings well broken up on a clear, pearly white ground. The ears must be black and the color evenly spaced on the head and surrounding both eyes, with a white blaze between the eyes. Rich tan markings over the eyes, on cheeks, inside ears, and on underside of tail. Ruby—Whole-colored rich red. Black and Tan—Jet black with rich, bright tan markings over the eyes, on cheeks, inside ears, on chest, legs, and on underside of tail. Faults—Heavy ticking on Blenheims and Tricolors, white marks on Rubies or Black and Tans.

Gait—Free-moving and elegant in action, with good reach in front and sound, driving rear action. When viewed from the side, the movement exhibits a good length of stride, and viewed from front and rear it is straight and true, resulting from straight-boned fronts and properly made and muscled hindquarters.

Temperament—Gay, friendly, non-aggressive with no tendency toward nervousness or shyness. Bad temper, shyness, and meanness are not to be tolerated and are to be so severely penalized as to effectively remove the specimen from competition.

Approved Date: January 10, 1995
Effective Date: April 30, 1995

The Cavalier is short-coupled, with the neck flowing smoothly into sloping shoulders, the topline continuing level.

Terms

coarse: large-boned and heavily muscled

cow hocks: heels that point inward toward one another

feathering: long hair of the ears, legs, and tail

flank: well-laid back; shoulder blade angled as close to 45 degrees as possible in relation to vertical

hocks well-let-down: heels close to the ground

leather: the ear flap, not including fur

pasterns: wrists

point of buttock: the rearmost point of the pelvis

point of shoulder: the frontmost point of the angle formed by the shoulder and upper arm

short-coupled: short between the rib cage and thigh

sickle hocks: heels that never straighten when the dog moves

snipiness: overly weak or pointed muzzle

stifles well-turned: knees showing a good amount of curve when viewed from the side

stop: transition from the backskull to muzzle

throatiness: excess skin under the neck

ticking: small dots of color

undershot: lower incisors protrude in front of upper incisors

weedy: small-boned and lacking muscles

well-sprung: somewhat rounded rib cage

whole-colored: no white

withers: the highest point of the shoulder

The King and I

After finally choosing your Cavalier pup, it's only natural to want to bring it home right away. But not so fast! It will be a lot easier to puppy-proof your home now than it will be when your tail-wagging scalawag is underfoot undoing everything as fast as you can do it! So channel your excitement and make sure everything is perfect before the homecoming. Just as much preparation needs to be made for welcoming an adult Cavalier.

If you are contemplating bringing your pup home as a Christmas present, think again. The heartwarming scene you may have imagined—the children discovering the puppy asleep amongst other gifts beneath the tree is not realistic. The real scene is more often that of a crying, confused puppy who may have vented its anxiety on the other gifts and left you some additional "gifts" of its own beneath the tree! Don't bring a new puppy into the excitement of Christmas morning. Not only does this add to what is bound to be a very confusing and intimidating transition for your Cavalier, but a puppy should not be expected to compete with all the toys the children may be receiving. At this crucial time every pup needs the undivided attention of its new family. Instead, a photograph or videotape of your special Cavalier-to-be or a stocking of puppy paraphernalia should provide sufficient surprise and give the whole family time to prepare.

A Cav's Home Is His Castle

The Cavalier can thrive in either an apartment or a house, as long as you do your part to make both your dog and your home safe. Even the mild-mannered Cavalier can make mistakes; rather than tempt such accidents, you will find that life with any dog is much easier if you make certain concessions and take certain precautions.

Outside: Unless you plan to walk your dog on a leash every time you take it outdoors, a secure fence should be your priority safety item. In today's world of automobiles and suburbs, a loose dog is at best an unwelcome visitor, and, more often, a dead

Buckle, choke, and martingale collars.

dog. The Cavalier seems unable to comprehend that anything could harm it, and so will stand trustingly in the path of a speeding car.

Your fence must not only be strong enough to keep your dog in, but to keep stray dogs out. This is why the "invisible fences" that keep your dog within are less than optimal, especially for small dogs. These barriers work only with a dog that is wearing a special shock collar that is activated by the buried boundary wire. They can't keep out stray dogs that aren't wearing such a collar.

Dangers can still loom within the yard. If you leave your Cavalier alone in your yard, lock your gate and take precautions against making your defenseless friend a target for thieves. Check for poisonous plants, bushes with sharp, broken branches at Cavalier eye level, and trees with dead branches or heavy fruits in danger of falling. If you have a pool, be aware that, although dogs are natural swimmers, a little Cavalier cannot pull itself up a swimming pool wall and can drown.

Inside: The first step in dog-proofing your home is to do everything you would to baby-proof your home. Get down at puppy level and see what dangers beckon.
• Puppies love to chew electrical cords and even lick outlets. These can result in death from shock, severe burns, and loss of jaw and tongue tissue. Hide cords behind furniture, and coat those you can't hide with an antichew preparation.
• Jumping up on an unstable object (such as a bookcase) could cause it to come crashing down, perhaps crushing the puppy.
• Do not allow the puppy near the edges of high decks, balconies, or staircases. Use temporary plastic fencing or chicken wire in dangerous areas.

Household Killers
• rodent, snail, and insect baits
• antifreeze
• household cleaners
• toilet fresheners
• drugs
• chocolate (especially baker's chocolate)
• nuts, bolts, pennies
• pins, needles, and anything else in a sewing basket
• chicken bones or any bone that could be swallowed

• Doors can be a danger area. Everyone in your family must be made to understand the danger of slamming a door, which could catch a small dog and break a leg—or worse. Use doorstops to ensure that the wind does not blow doors suddenly shut, or that the puppy does not go behind a door to play. This can be a danger, because the gap on the hinged side of the door can catch and break a little leg if the door is closed. Be especially cautious with swinging doors; a puppy may try to push one open, become caught, try to back out, and strangle. Clear glass doors may not be seen, and the puppy could be injured running into them. Never close a garage door with a Cavalier running about. Finally, doors leading to unfenced outdoor areas should be kept securely shut.

As much as your Cavalier may try to be good, it's your duty to remove it from temptation. A pup left alone can be an accomplished one-dog demolition team. Leather furniture is the world's biggest rawhide chewy, and wicker can provide hours of chewing enjoyment (and danger from splintering). Puppies particularly like to chew items that carry your scent. Shoes, eyeglasses, and clothing must be kept out of the youngster's reach. Remove books and papers. No need for a

If you are sure your Cav pup can't get into it—it can!

Your welcome basket should be prepared before your puppy arrives.

costly paper shredder when you have a puppy!

Your carpets can be covered with small washable rugs until your puppy is housebroken. If you use an X-pen (exercise pen), cover the floor beneath it with thick plastic (an old shower curtain works well), and then add towels or washable rugs for traction and absorbency.

The Homecoming Kit

It's not really true that "all you need is love" (but you'll need lots of that, too)! Best sources for accessories are large pet stores, dog shows, and discount pet catalogs. Here is your welcome basket checklist.

• Buckle collar: for wearing around the house.
• Choke or martingale collar: safer for walking on lead.
• Leash: nylon, web, or leather—never chain! An adjustable show lead is good for puppies.
• Lightweight retractable leash: better for older adult; be sure not to drop the leash as it can retract toward the pup and frighten it.
• Stainless steel flat-bottomed food and water bowls: avoid plastic; it can cause allergic reactions and hold germs.
• Cage: just large enough for an adult to stand up in without having to lower its head.
• Exercise pen: tall enough that an adult can't jump over.
• Toys: fleece-type toys, balls, stuffed animals, stuffed socks. Make sure no parts of toys, including squeakers or plastic eyes, can be pulled off and swallowed.
• Chewbones: the equivalent of a teething ring for babies; nylon chewbones are preferable to rawhide.
• Antichew preparations, such as Bitter Apple. The unpleasant taste dissuades pups from chewing on sprayed items.

• Baby gate(s): better than a shut door for placing parts of your home off limits. Do not use the accordion style, which could choke a dog.
• Brush and comb.
• Nail clippers.
• Poop scoop: Two piece rake-type is best for grass.
• Dog shampoo (see page 53 for choices).
• First aid kit (see page 60 for contents).
• Food: start with the same food the pup is currently eating.
• Dog bed: a round fleece-lined cat bed is heavenly, but you can also use the bottom of a plastic cage, or any cozy box with padding. Wicker will most likely be chewed to shreds.
• Camera and film! (telephoto lens is a big help.)

Puppies and adults will need plenty of toys.

The Den

Just as you find peace and security as you sink into your own bed at night, your pup needs a place that it can call its own, a place it can seek out whenever the need for rest and solitude arises. That place is its cage. Used properly, your Cavalier will come to think of its cage not as a place to be kept in, but as a place where others are kept out!

A cage (or crate) is the canine equivalent of an infant's crib. It is a place for naptime, a place where you can leave your pup without worry of its hurting itself or your home. It is not a place for punishment, nor is it a storage box for your dog when you're through playing with it. Place the cage in a corner of a quiet room, but not too far from the rest of the family. Place the pup in the cage when it begins to fall asleep and it will become accustomed to using it as its bed. Be sure to place a soft blanket in the bottom. And by taking the pup upon awakening directly from the cage to the outdoors, the cage will be one of the handiest housebreaking aids at your disposal.

An exercise pen (or "X-pen") fulfills many of the same functions as a cage. X-pens are transportable, folding wire "playpens" for dogs, typically about 4 feet by 4 feet (1.3 m x 1.3 m). X-pens are the perfect solution when you must be gone for a long time, because the pup can relieve itself on paper in one corner, sleep on a soft bed in the

Decide now if you will allow your Cavalier on furniture.

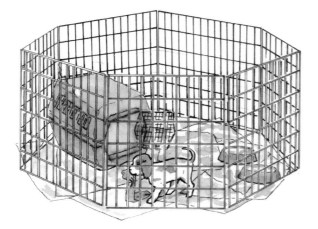

A safe haven for puppy and home: the X-pen.

other, and frolic with its toys all over! It's like having a little yard inside. The X-pen provides a safe time-out area when you just need some quiet time for yourself. But before leaving your pup in an X-pen, make sure that it cannot jump or climb out. Covers are available for incorrigible escapees.

Don't let your puppy have the run of the entire house. Choose an easily puppy-proofed room where you spend a lot of time, preferably one that is close to a door leading outside. Kitchens and dens are usually ideal. When you must leave your dog for some time, you may wish to place it in a cage, X-pen, secure room, or outdoor kennel. Bathrooms have the disadvantage of being so confining and isolated that puppies may become destructive; garages have the disadvantage of also housing many poisonous items.

The scoop: The least glamorous, yet essential, item on your list is the poop scoop. What goes in must come out, at best in your own yard. Too many dog owners never step foot in their own backyards because of dog poop. Dogs raised in unclean yards

grow used to stepping in feces and will continue to do so with reckless abandon their entire lives, an especially disgusting trait if your dog sleeps in your bed or tends to jump up on you. Start early and keep your yard meticulously scooped, except for a sample pile in the area you wish the dog to continue using as its toilet area. Don't make your Cavalier live in a mine field.

A Red Carpet Welcome

Schedule your new pup's homecoming during a period when you will have several days to spend at home. But don't make the mistake of spending every moment with the new dog. Accustom the youngster to short times away from you, so that when you do leave the house the puppy won't be too upset.

Your pup will learn a new name quickly if it means food or fun is on the way. Be careful about the name you choose; for example, "Nomad" sounds like both "no" and "bad," and could confuse a dog. Test your chosen name to be sure that it does not sound like a reprimand or command.

When you get home, put the puppy on lead and carry it to the spot you have decided will be its toilet area. Note that the toilet area is not the play area. Once the puppy relieves itself, praise and give it a tidbit, then take it to another area of the yard to let it explore a little. Your pup will probably be hungry, so offer it a small meal once inside. Once the puppy has eaten, it will probably have to relieve itself again, so take it back out to the toilet area and remember to praise and give a tidbit for a job well done. When your pup begins to act sleepy, place it in its cage so that it knows this is its special bed. A stuffed toy, ticking clock, or even plastic milk carton filled with warm water may help alleviate some of the anxiety of being left alone. You may wish to place the cage in your bedroom for this first night so that the puppy may be comforted by your presence. Remember, this is the scariest thing that has ever happened in your puppy's short life; it has been uprooted from the security of a mother, littermates, and loving breeder, so you must be comforting and reassuring on this crucial first night.

The first day with you is not the time for all the neighbors to come visiting. You want your pup to know who its new family members will be, and more people will only add to the youngster's confusion. Nor is it the time for rough-and-tumble play, which could scare the puppy. Introductions to other family pets might also be better postponed. Why make a confusing and stressful experience even more overwhelming?

Cradle the pup under its chest and rear, and hold it securely next to your own body.

Creating a Civilized Housedog

Your pup now faces the transition from canine litter member to human family member. Every day will be full of novel experiences and new rules. Your pup is naturally inquisitive and will need you to guide it toward becoming a well-mannered member of the household.

Off-limits training: Before bringing your puppy home you should decide what parts of your home will be off limits. Make sure that every family member understands the rules, and that they understand that sneaking the puppy onto off-limit furniture, for example, is not doing the puppy any favor at all. Your puppy will naturally want to explore every nook and cranny of your house. Part of the pup's exploratory tools are its teeth, and any chewed items left in its wake are your fault, not your pup's—you are the one who should have known better. Harsh corrections are no more effective than a tap on the nose along with a firm "No" and removal of the item. If you come across one of your cherished items chewed to bits and feel compelled to lash out, go ahead—hit yourself in the head a few times for slipping up. It may teach you a lesson!

Cavaliers naturally consider your chairs and sofas to be their thrones, but if you don't want them on the furniture keep them off from the beginning. Don't pick the pup up to sit on your lap; instead, sit on the floor with it. Don't fling the pup off furniture or use mousetraps on furniture surfaces, because both practices are dangerous and absolutely a bad idea unless you like emergency visits to the vet. There are several more humane items (available through pet catalogs) that emit a loud tone when a dog jumps on furniture, but these should not be necessary if you train your young puppy gently and consistently from the beginning.

Housebreaking

Because dogs are creatures of habit, housebreaking is more a matter of prevention than correction. To avoid accidents, learn to predict when your puppy will have to relieve itself. Immediately after awakening and soon after heavy drinking or playing, your puppy will urinate. You will probably have to carry a younger baby outside to get it to the toilet area on time. Right after eating, or if nervous, your puppy will have to defecate. Circling, whining, sniffing, and generally acting worried usually signals that defecation is imminent. Even if the puppy starts to relieve itself, quickly but calmly scoop the pup up and carry it outside (the surprise of being picked up will usually cause the puppy to stop in midstream, so to speak). You can also clap your hands or make a loud noise to startle the pup so that it stops. You can add a firm "No," but yelling and

"Who me? Get into trouble?" You bet!

swatting are actually detrimental. When the puppy does relieve itself in its outside toilet, remember to heap on the praise and let your Cavalier pup know how pleased you are. Adding a food treat really gets the point across. Keep some in a jar near the door and always accompany your pup outside so that you can reward it.

Puppies tend to defecate and urinate in areas where they can smell that they have relieved themselves before. This is why it is critical never to let the pup have an accident indoors; if it does, clean and deodorize the spot thoroughly and block the pup's access to that area. Use a pet deodorizer cleaner, and never use one containing ammonia. Ammonia is a component of urine, so using an ammonia cleaner is like posting a sign that says "go here"!

The number one housebreaking mistake made by most puppy owners is to give their puppies too much unsupervised freedom in the house. All canines have a natural desire to avoid soiling their den area. As soon as young wolves are able to walk, they will teeter out of their den to relieve themselves away from their bedding. Since you are using a cage for your puppy's den, your Cavalier will naturally try to avoid soiling it. The den area is considerably smaller than your house, however, and it will take some training before your pup extends the notion of den to your entire home.

Puppies have very weak control over their bowels, so that if you don't take them to their elimination area often, they may not be able to avoid soiling. Puppies, like babies, have to eliminate a lot. You can't just stick them in a cage all day while you are at work and think you won't return home to a messy cage and messy pup. A rule of thumb is that a puppy can, at most, hold its bowels for as many hours as the pup is months old. This means that a three-month old can hold itself for three hours. If the pup is forced to stay in a cage longer, so that it can't hold itself and has to soil the cage, you are setting the stage for a big problem. Once it gets used to eliminating in its cage, it may continue. Further, if the cage is too large, the puppy may simply step away from the area it sleeps in and relieve itself at the other end of the cage. An overly large cage can be divided with a secure barrier until the puppy is larger or housebroken.

The number two housebreaking mistake made by dog owners is overuse of punishment. Even if you catch your dog in the act, overly enthusiastic correction tends only to teach the dog not to relieve itself in your presence, even when outside. This is why you should reward with a tidbit when the pup does relieve itself outside. Punishment doesn't make clear what is desired behavior, but reward makes it clear very quickly. Punishing a dog for a mess it has made earlier is totally fruitless; it only succeeds in convincing the dog that every once in a while, for no apparent reason, you are apt to go insane and attack it. It is a perfect recipe for ruining a trusting relationship. That "guilty" look you may think your dog is exhibiting is really fear that you have once again lost your mind.

The number three housebreaking mistake owners make is to open the door and push the pup outside by itself. After five minutes, the pup is let back in and promptly relieves itself on the rug. Bad dog? No, bad owner. Chances are the pup spent its time outside trying to get back inside to its owner. Puppies do not like to be alone, and knowing you are on the other side of the door makes the outside unappealing. If the weather was bad, it probably huddled against the door so it wouldn't miss when it was

A friend can sometimes help problems associated with boredom or separation anxiety.

again opened. The solution? You must go outside with the pup every time. Don't take it for a walk, don't play with it, simply go with it to its relief area, say "hurry up" (the most popular choice of command words), and be ready to praise and perhaps give a treat when the pup does its deed. Then you can play or go back inside.

If you cannot be with your puppy for an extended period, you may wish to leave it outside (weather permitting) so that it will not be forced to have an indoor accident. If this is not possible, you may have to paper train your puppy. Place newspapers on the far side of the room (or X-pen), away from the puppy's bed or water bowl; near a door to the outside is best. Place the puppy on the papers as soon as it starts to relieve itself.

A better option is to use sod squares instead of newspapers. Place the sod on a plastic sheet, and when soiled, take it outside and hose it off. By using sod, you are training the pup to relieve itself on the same surface it

Separation anxiety is characterized by lapses in housebreaking, nervous behavior, and destruction around doors and windows, particularly chewed and scratched walls, door jams, and rugs.

should eventually use outside. Place the soiled squares outside in the area that you want your dog to use.

As soon as you are hopeful your precocious puppy is housebroken, it will take a giant step backward and convince you there is no link between its brain and bowels. Most people have unrealistic expectations of their dog's ability to become housebroken, based in part upon friends' boasting about their little genius that was housebroken at two days of age or something similarly ludicrous. No matter how wonderful and smart your Cavalier is, it probably will not have full control over its elimination until it is around six months of age, and probably won't be reliably housebroken until a year old— or more! Keep up your training and things really will get better.

If things don't get better, or if your previously housebroken adult Cavalier soils the house, consider the following possible causes:

• Some dogs defecate or urinate as an expression of separation anxiety; you must treat the anxiety to cure the symptom. Dogs that mess their cage when left in it are usually suffering from separation anxiety or anxiety about being closed in a cage. Other telltale signs of anxiety-produced elimination are drooling, scratching, and escape-oriented behavior. You need to treat separation anxiety (see page 32) and start cage training over, placing the pup in it for a short period of time and working up gradually to longer times. Some dogs that suffer from cage anxiety but not separation anxiety do better if left loose in a dog-proof room.

• Submissive dogs, especially young females, may urinate upon greeting you; punishment only makes this "submissive urination" worse. For these dogs, keep greetings calm, don't bend over or otherwise dominate the dog, and usually this can be outgrown as the dog gains more confidence.

• Sometimes a housebroken dog will be forced to soil the house because of a bout of diarrhea, and afterwards will continue to soil in the same area. If this happens, restrict the dog from that area and revert to basic housebreaking lessons once again. Deodorize the area with an enzymatic cleaner (free of ammonia).

• Dogs sometimes lose control because of a bladder infection; several small urine spots (especially if bloody or dark) are a sign that a trip to the veterinarian is needed. In fact, a physical examination is warranted any time a formerly housebroken dog begins to soil the house.

• Older dogs simply do not have the bladder control that they had as youngsters; paper training or a doggy door is the best solution for them.

• Older spayed females may "dribble," ask your veterinarian about drug therapy.

• Male dogs may "lift their leg" inside the house as a means of marking it as theirs. Castration will often solve this problem as long as it is performed before the habit has become established; otherwise diligent deodorizing and the use of some dog-deterring odorants (available at pet stores) may help. A tube-shaped doggy diaper, available at dog shows, can help incorrigible males.

Royal Pains

One glance into those big innocent eyes and it is hard to believe that your Cavalier could ever do anything wrong. But even the best of dogs with the best of owners can sometimes do the worst of things. Sometimes the behavior is so intolerable that owners can no longer cope with the dog, and either give it up or euthanize it. Great strides have been made in recent years in canine behavioral therapy. Before despairing consult a certified canine behaviorist (not a local dog trainer), who may employ a combination of conditioning and drug therapy to achieve a cure.

Misuse of punishment is a major cause of continuing problems. If punishment doesn't work the first time, why do owners think that it will work the second, third, or fourth time?

Jumping up: Puppies naturally greet their mother and other adult dogs by licking them around the corners of their mouth. This behavior translates to humans, but to reach your face they need to jump up on you. Sometimes owners love this display of affection, but not when they are all dressed up or when company comes. But you can't expect your Cavalier to know the difference. Instead, teach your dog to sit and stay, and then be sure to kneel down to its level for greetings. When your Cav does jump up, simply say "no" and step backward, so that its paws

Teach your Cavalier to stay on the ground for greetings by kneeling down to its level.

meet only air. Teaching your dog a special command that lets it know it's OK to jump up (when you're in your grubby clothes) can actually help it differentiate.

Shutting your dog in another room when guests arrive will only make it more crazed to greet people, and ultimately worsen the problem. The more people it gets a chance to greet politely, the less excited it will be about meeting new people, and the less inclined it will be to jump up. Have your guests kneel and greet your sitting Cavalier.

Barking: Having a doggy doorbell can be handy, but there is a difference between a dog that will warn you of a suspicious stranger and one that will warn you of the presence of oxygen in the air. The surest way to make your neighbors dislike your dog is to let it create a racket. Allow your Cav to bark momentarily at strangers, and then call it to you and praise it for quiet behavior, distracting it with an obedience exercise if need be.

Isolated dogs will often bark as a means of getting attention and alleviating loneliness. Even if the attention gained includes punishment, the dog will continue to bark in order to obtain the temporary presence of the owner. The simplest solution is to move the dog's quarters to a less isolated location. For example, if barking occurs when your pup is put to bed, move its bed into your bedroom. If this is not possible, the pup's quiet behavior must be rewarded by the owner's presence, working up to gradually longer and longer periods. The distraction of a special chew toy, given only at bedtime, may help alleviate barking. The pup that must spend the day home alone is a greater challenge. Again, the simplest solution is to change the situation, perhaps by adding another animal—a good excuse to get two Cavaliers! But warning: Some Cavaliers also like to bark when playing!

Digging: All breeds of dogs dig. It is a natural canine behavior, and the only cure is to give your aspiring miner a lot of exercise and a lot of supervision. Better yet, fence off those parts of the yard that you absolutely can't tolerate being turned into a moonscape, and direct your dog to its own special sandbox. Remedies based on harsh corrections are not successful.

Home destruction: Home destruction is one of the most common, and commonly misunderstood, Cavalier behavior problems. The Cavalier is an extremely devoted dog, and its owners are typically extremely devoted people. They chose a Cavalier in part because of the breed's desire to be close to its people. The problem is, for many dogs, the people go off and desert them on a regular basis. Dogs are highly social animals, and being left alone is an extremely stressful condition for many of them. They react by becoming agitated and trying to escape from confinement. Perhaps they reason that if they can just get out of the house they will be reunited with their people. The telltale signature of a dog suffering from separation anxiety is that most of its destructive behavior is focused around doors and windows. Most owners believe the dog is "spiting" them for leaving it, and punish the dog. But dogs never destroy out of spite. Punishment is ineffective because it actually increases the anxiety of the dog, as it comes to both look forward to and dread its owner's return.

The proper therapy is treatment of the dog's fear of being left alone. This is done by leaving the dog alone for very short periods of time and gradually working to longer periods, taking care never to allow the dog to become anxious during any session. When you must leave the dog for long periods during the conditioning program, leave it in a different part of the house than the one in which the conditioning sessions take place, so that you don't undo all your work by letting the dog become overstressed by your long absence.

In either case, when you return home, no matter what the condition of the home, greet the dog calmly or even ignore it for a few minutes, to emphasize the point that being left was really no big deal. Then have the dog perform a simple trick or obedience exercise so that you have an excuse to praise it. It takes a lot of patience, and often a whole lot of self-control, but it's not fair to you or your dog to let this situation continue. Separation anxiety is really a type of fear: the fear of being left alone.

Puppies are natural demolition dogs, and the best cure is adulthood.

Adult dogs still may dig or destroy items through frustration or boredom. The best way to deal with these dogs is to provide both physical interaction (such as chasing a ball) and mental interaction (such as practicing a few simple obedience commands) on a daily basis.

Fearfulness: Despite their generally fearless attitude, Cavaliers can develop phobias and other fears. Fearfulness can be prevented to a great extent by early socialization of your pup. Once your pup is vaccinated, take it on outings where it will meet friendly people and well-behaved dogs. Go to the park, puppy kindergarten classes, or for walks in the neighborhood. Make each encounter a positive one, and never push your dog into situations that might overwhelm it.

Fear of thunder is a common problem in older dogs. Try to avoid it by acting cheerful when a thunderstorm strikes, and play with your dog or give it a tidbit. Once a dog develops a thunder phobia, try to find a recording of a thunderstorm. Play it at a very low level and reward your dog for calm behavior. Gradually increase the intensity and duration of the recording.

Another common fear is a fear of strangers. Never force a dog that is afraid of people to be petted by somebody it doesn't know; it in no way helps the dog overcome its fear and is a good way for the stranger to get bitten. Strangers should be asked to ignore shy dogs, even when approached by the dog. Dogs seem to fear the attention of a stranger more than they fear the strangers themselves. When the dog gets braver, have the stranger offer it a tidbit, at first while not even looking at the dog. A program of gradual desensitization, with the dog exposed to the frightening person or thing and then rewarded for calm behavior, is time-consuming but the best way to alleviate any fear.

Allow a fearful dog to approach and investigate a stranger from behind, with the stranger ignoring the dog.

Never coddle your dog when it acts afraid, because it reinforces the behavior. It is always useful if your Cavalier knows a few simple commands; performing these exercises correctly gives you a reason to praise the dog and also increases the dog's sense of security because it knows what is expected of it. Whether it is a fear of strangers, dogs, car rides, thunder, or being left alone, the concept is the same: never hurry, and never push the dog to the point that it is afraid.

Aggression: In some breeds aggression often results from a dog's attempts to dominate its owners. This is virtually never the case in Cavaliers. Aggression is uncommon in Cavaliers but, when it does occur, it is more likely to result from fear. A scared dog with no route of escape will often bark, growl, or bite out of perceived self-defense. Unlike in humans, where direct eye contact is seen as a sign of sincerity, staring a dog directly in the eye is interpreted by the dog as a threat. It can cause a fearful dog to bite.

HOW-TO:
Speaking the King's English

Dubbed "man's best friend," our dogs are expected to understand us without our bothering to learn their language. With very little effort, you can meet your Cavalier halfway. Like their wolf ancestors, Cavaliers depend upon facial expressions and body language in social interactions.

• A yawn is often a sign of nervousness. Drooling and panting can indicate extreme nervousness (as well as car-sickness).

• A wagging tail, lowered head, and exposed teeth upon greeting is a sign of submission.

• The combination of a lowered body, wagging tucked tail, urination, and perhaps even rolling over is a sign of extreme submission.

• The combination of exposed teeth, a high, rigidly held tail, raised hackles, very upright

The wagging tail and raised rear end is an invitation to play, but the other dog is too submissive to join in.

posture, stiff-legged gait, direct stare, forward-raised ears, and perhaps lifting its leg to urinate indicates very dominant, possibly threatening behavior.

• The combination of a wagging tail, front legs and elbows on the ground and rear in the air, is the classic "play-bow" position, and is an invitation for a game.

Your Cavalier not only speaks a different language from yours, but it lives in a different sensory world.

Olfaction: The dog's scenting ability is so vastly superior

to ours that it is as though we were blind in comparison. The dog can seek out hidden objects and animals, follow a trail for miles, and distinguish between individuals by scent. The Cavalier has not lost its keen sense of smell, and is an adept scenter.

Taste: Dogs also have a well-developed sense of taste, and have most of the same taste receptors that we do. Research has shown that they prefer meat (not exactly earth-shaking news) and, while there are many individual differences, the average dog prefers beef, pork, lamb, chicken, and horsemeat, in that order.

Dogs have sugar receptors similar to ours, which explains why many have a sweet tooth. But their perception of artificial sweeteners is not like ours; these seem to taste bitter to dogs.

Vision: The dog's eye is superior when it comes to seeing in very dim light. The eye-shine you may see from your dog's eyes at night is from a reflective structure (the tapetum lucidum) that serves to increase its ability to see in very dim light, and the dog has a greater

The nervous dog will pant, drool, and shake, as well as hold its ears and tail down. The threatening dog stands high and stiff-legged, tail held erect, and with an intense stare.

proportion of the type of retinal cells (rods) that are highly sensitive to dim light than do humans.

No dogs see the world with as much detail or color as do humans. The dog's sense of color is like that of what is commonly called a "color-blind" person, which is not really blind to color at all. That is, they confuse similar shades of yellow-green, yellow, orange, and red, but can readily see and discriminate blue, indigo, and violet from all other colors and each other.

Hearing: Dogs can hear much higher tones than can humans, and so can be irritated by high hums from your TV or from those ultrasonic flea collars. The high-pitched "dog whistles" so popular years ago emit a tone higher than humans can hear, but well within the dog's range. Ultrasonic training devices now available emit a high-frequency sound inaudible to us, but irritating and distracting to dogs.

While you admire a beautiful vista, your Cavalier is much more likely to be enthralled by the scent of a long gone animal.

Pain: Scientific research indicates that dogs have a well-developed sense of pain. Many dogs are amazingly stoic, however, and their ability to deal with pain is not totally understood at present. Because a dog may not be able to express that it is in pain, you must be alert to changes in your dog's demeanor. A stiff gait, low head carriage, reluctance to get up, irritability, dilated pupils, whining, or limping are all indications that your dog is in pain.

Even angels need guidance.

sitting and staying—in the presence of guests, and by having guests offer the dog a treat. A drastic measure is to withhold attention from the dog except in the presence of guests or baby, so that the dog associates being with them as something that brings itself attention and rewards. Of course, it should hardly need mention that no baby or child should be allowed to play roughly with or tease your Cavalier; one could hardly blame a small dog that growls or bites out of self-defense, but one could blame its owner for letting the situation develop.

Cavaliers get along well with other dogs, but occasionally housemates will fight for dominance or the owner's attention. Your best way to help is by allowing one dog to be clearly dominant. Don't help or coddle the "underdog," you will be hurting it in the long run. The dominant dog can interpret your favoring of the underdog as though its dominance was being threatened, and it may attack the subordinate dog.

Dogs that are hustled out of the room when guests arrive, or out of the family activities when a new baby arrives, will sometimes bite out of resentment. Teach your Cavalier to look forward to guests and children by rewarding proper behavior—such as

When introducing new dogs, it is best if both are taken to a neutral site so that territoriality does not provoke aggression. Two people walking the dogs beside each other as they would on a regular walk is an ideal way for dogs to accept each other.

The Courteous Cavalier

As an integral member of your family, your Cavalier will need guidance to be a proper little lady or gentleman. Young Cavaliers are natural followers, not leaders. They will elect you as their leader and will expect you to guide them. Don't let them down.

Head of the Class

Dog obedience classes are a good idea for several reasons:
• They keep you motivated to stay on schedule.
• They are a source of training advice that can tell you what you are doing wrong as no book could ever do.
• They provide an environment filled with distractions that are good for polishing your exercises.
• They provide a safe venue for your Cavalier's socialization with dogs and people.
• And where else could you have so much fun showing off your little genius?

Dog obedience classes can also be a bad idea. They will be a big disappointment if you think you can drop your dog off and it will return to you totally trained. You want your dog to mind you, not a trainer. A trainer who thinks all dogs need to be dominated and treated like crazed headstrong beasts is a disaster. But how can you know about a class or instructor ahead of time?

One way is to attend a dog show or obedience trial (contact the AKC for dates and locations) and find local people whose dogs are in competition. Be on the lookout especially for other "soft" breeds, and watch how their owners train their dogs. If you like what you see, find out what class they attend and what techniques the class advocates. Finally, try to sit in on a class and watch how the dogs are treated. If rough methods are used, keep on looking.

Dog training methods have changed little through the years—but they should have. Traditional dog training methods based on force are the least successful and most widespread. The problem with training by force is that it

The courteous Cavalier is a pleasure both at home and abroad.

Use a back scratcher to extend your arm's length so you can touch your Cav without having to bend over. By stringing your leash through a hollow tube (such as PVC pipe) you can lower its pivoting point, which will give you much more directional control when guiding a small dog.

relies upon punishment as a means of telling the dog what not to do, but it is seldom successful in telling the dog what it should do.

Food for Thought

Many years ago the idea was propagated that dogs should never be trained with food. Yet professional animal trainers and animal learning scientists all knew that food training produced excellent results, because food tells the animal what behaviors are correct. Only recently has food-motivated training become accepted in training the family dog, and owners are finding that dogs learn faster, mind more reliably, work more eagerly, and have a more trusting dog-owner relationship.

At first food is used to guide the dog by the nose until it is in the desired position, and then to reward the dog

when it is in place. After the dog knows what is expected, the food is held out of sight and only given to the dog when it has performed correctly. Ultimately the dog is weaned from getting a food reward each time, but still gets one every once in a while. Such a randomized payoff schedule has been shown to be very effective with both animals and humans (as in slot machine payoffs!)

The idea of bribing our dogs with food runs counter to the idealized picture of Lassie obeying out of pure goodness and love. But the real Lassie, of course, was performing for food. Dog owners have been told for years that the dog should work for praise only, but praise alone is not really a terribly strong motivator for most dogs. Praise can become a stronger motivator by always praising immediately before the food reward is given. In this way it becomes a secondary reinforcer, much as a gold star on a child's schoolwork gains reinforcing value because it has been paired with other positive reinforcement. Eventually the dog can be weaned from the food and will come to work in large part for praise, but food should still be given as reward intermittently.

The Right Way to Train

Cavaliers are very amenable to training, but they respond best to gentle techniques. Do both you and your dog a favor and don't necessarily listen to your next-door neighbor's training advice or use the same techniques your grandparents (or even your parents) used. Use the methods the professionals use, and you will be astounded by what your Cavalier can learn.

• **Guide, don't force:** Cavaliers already want to please you; your job is to simply show them the way. Forcing them can distract them or intimidate them, actually slowing down learning.

• **Correct, don't punish:** Such methods as striking, shaking, choking, and hanging have been touted by some (stupid) trainers: Do not try them! These methods are extremely dangerous, counterproductive, and cruel; they have no place in the training of a beloved family member. Plus, they don't work.

• **Correct and be done with it:** Owners sometimes try to make this "a correction the dog will remember" by ignoring or chastising the dog for the rest of the day. The dog may indeed remember that its owner was upset, but it will not remember why. The dog can only relate its present behavior to your actions.

• **You get what you ask for:** Dogs repeat actions that bring them rewards, whether you intend this connection or not. Letting your Cav out of its cage to make it quit whining might work momentarily, but in the long run you will end up with a dog that whines incessantly every time you put it in a cage. Make sure you reward only those behaviors you want to see more often.

• **Mean what you say:** Sometimes a puppy can be awfully cute when it misbehaves, or sometimes your hands are full, and sometimes you just aren't sure what you want from your dog. But lapses in consistency are ultimately unfair to the dog. If you feed your begging dog from the table "just this one time," you have taught it that while begging may not always result in a handout, you never know, it just might pay off tonight. In other words, you have taught your dog to beg.

• **Say what you mean:** Your Cavalier takes its commands literally. If you have taught that "Down" means to lie down, then what must the dog think when you yell "Down" to tell it to get off the sofa where it was already lying down? Or "Sit down" when you mean "Sit"? If "Stay" means not to move until given a release word and you say

Use food to guide your Cavalier's head backwards and slightly up. If you position its rear end next to a wall, it will have to sit in order to reach the treat.

"Stay here" as you leave the house for work, do you really want your dog to sit by the door all day until you get home?

• **Train before meals:** Your Cavalier will work better if its stomach is not full, and will be more responsive to food rewards. Never try to train a sleepy, tired, or hot dog.

• **Happy endings:** Begin and end each training session with something the dog can do well. And keep sessions short and fun—no longer than 10 to 15 minutes. Dogs have short attention spans and you will notice that after about 15 minutes their performance will begin to suffer unless a lot of play is involved. To continue to train a tired or bored dog will result in the training of bad habits, resentment in the dog, and frustration for the trainer. Especially when training a young puppy, or when you only have

Keep a light leash on your Cav when first teaching the "Stay."

one or two different exercises to practice, quit while you are ahead! Keep your Cavalier wanting more.

• **Name, command, action!** The first ingredient in any command is your dog's name. You probably spend a good deal of your day talking, with very few words intended as commands for your dog. So warn your dog that this talk is directed toward it.

Many trainers make the mistake of saying the command word at the same time that they are placing the dog into position. This is incorrect. The command comes immediately before the desired action or position. The crux of training is anticipation: the dog comes to anticipate that after hearing a command, it will be induced to perform some action, and it will eventually perform this action without further assistance from you. On the other hand, when the command and action come at the same time, not only does the dog tend to pay more attention to your action of placing it in position, and less attention to the command word, but the command word loses its predictive value for the dog. Remember: Name, command, action, reward!

• **Once is enough:** Repeating a command over and over, or shouting it louder and louder, never helped anyone, dog or human, understand what is expected. Your Cavalier is not hard of hearing.

• **Think like a dog:** Dogs live in the present; if you punish them they can only assume it is for their behavior at the time of punishment. So if you discover a mess, drag your dog to it from its nap in the other room, and scold, the dog's impression will be that either it is being scolded for napping, or that its owner is mentally unstable. In many ways dogs are like young children; they act to gratify themselves, and they often do so without thinking ahead to consequences. But unlike young children, dogs cannot understand human language (except for those words you teach them), so you cannot explain to them that their actions of five minutes earlier were bad. Remember timing is everything in

You can teach the "Sit," "Down," and "Stay" on a table top.

a correction. If you discover your dog in the process of having an "accident," and snatch the dog up and deposit it outside, and then yell "No," your dog can only conclude that you have yelled "No" to it for eliminating outside. Correct timing would be "No," quickly take the dog outside, and then reward it once it eliminates outside. In this way you have corrected the dog's undesired behavior and helped the dog understand desired behavior.

• **The best-laid plans:** Finally, nothing will ever go as perfectly as it seems to in all the training instructions. But although there may be setbacks, you can train your dog, as long as you remember to be consistent, firm, gentle, realistic, and, most of all, patient.

Training equipment: Equipment for training should include a six-foot (2 m) and a 20-foot (6.6 m) lightweight lead. For puppies it is convenient to use one of the lightweight, adjustable-size show leads. Most Cavaliers can be trained with a buckle collar, but a choke collar is also an acceptable choice as long as you know how to use it correctly.

A choke collar is not for choking! In fact, it is more correctly termed a slip collar. The proper way to administer a correction with a choke collar is with a gentle snap, then immediate release. If you think of the point of the correction as being to startle the dog by the sound of the chain links moving, rather than to choke or in any way hurt your dog, you will be correcting with the right level of force. The choke collar is placed on the dog so that the ring with the lead attached comes up around the left side of the dog's neck, and through the other ring. If put on backwards, it will not release itself after being tightened (since you will be on the right side of your dog for most training). The choke collar should never be left on your Cavalier after a training session; there are too many

The correct placement of the choke collar is with the long end (to which the lead is attached) coming over the top of the dog's head from the dog's left to right side.

tragic cases where a choke collar really did earn its name after being snagged on a fence, bush, or even a playmate's tooth. Allowing a dog to run around wearing a choke collar is like allowing a child to run around wearing a hangman's noose.

What Every Savvy Cavvy Should Know

It's never too early or too late to start the education of your Cavalier. With a very young Cav, train for even shorter time periods. By the time your Cav pup (here named "Savannah") reaches 6 months of age, it should be familiar with the following commands:

Watch me: A common problem when training any dog is that the dog's attention is elsewhere. You can teach your dog to pay attention to you by teaching it the "watch me" command. Say "Savannah, watch me," and when she looks in your direction, give her a treat or other reward. Gradually require the dog to look at you for longer and longer periods before rewarding it. Teach "watch me" before going on to the other commands.

Sit: Because Cavs are already close to the ground, many of them virtually teach themselves to sit as a means of being more comfortable while looking up at you. But you can hasten the process by holding a tidbit above your puppy's eye level, saying "Savannah, sit," and then moving the tidbit toward your pup until it is slightly behind and above her eyes. You may have to keep a hand on her rump to prevent her from jumping up. When she begins to look up and bend her hind legs, praise, then offer the tidbit. Repeat this, requiring the dog to bend her legs more and more until she must be sitting before receiving praise.

Once the "Sit" is mastered, use food to lure your dog to the ground. You may have to keep a hand on its shoulders to prevent it from getting up.

Tip: Teach stationary exercises on a tabletop or other raised surface. This allows you to have eye contact with your dog and gives you a better vantage from which to help your dog learn.

To train your dog at your feet, extend your arm length with a back scratcher with which to guide and even pet your dog without having to bend over.

Stay: A dangerous habit of many dogs is to bolt through open doors, whether they be in the house or car. Teach your dog to sit and stay until given the release signal before walking through the front door or exiting your car.

Have your dog sit, then say "Stay" in a soothing voice (for commands in which the dog is not supposed to move, don't precede the command with the dog's name). If your Cav attempts to get up or lie down, gently but instantly place it back into position. Work up to a few seconds, give a release word ("OK!"), praise and give a tidbit. Next, step out (starting with your right foot) and turn to stand directly in front of your dog while it stays. Work up to longer times, but don't ask a young puppy to stay longer than 30 seconds. The object is not to push your dog to the limit, but to let it succeed. To do this you must be very patient, and you must add to your times and distances in very small increments. Finally, practice with the dog on lead by the front door or in the car. For a reward, take her for a walk!

Tip: Don't stare at your dog during the Stay, as this is perceived by dogs as a threat and often intimidates them so that they squirm out of position or creep to you submissively.

Come: Coming on command is more than a cute trick; it could save your dog's life. Your puppy probably already knows how to come; after all, it comes when it sees you with the food bowl, or perhaps with the leash or a favorite toy. You may have even used the word "Come" to get its attention then; if so, you have a head start. You want your puppy to respond to "Savannah, come" with the same enthusiasm she greets your setting down her supper; in other words, "Come" should always be associated with good things.

Never have your dog come to you and then scold it for something it has done. In the dog's mind it is being scolded for coming, not for any earlier misdeed. Most trainers teach "Come" only from a sitting position, but in real life the dog is seldom sitting when you want it to come. With the pup on lead, command "Savannah, come!" enthusiastically, and back or run away, luring her with the tidbit. When she reaches you, praise and reward her. When she seems to have the idea, attach a longer line to her, allow her to meander about, and in the midst of her investigations, call, run backwards, and reward. Eventually you can just stand still when you call. You should ultimately practice (on lead) in the presence of distractions, such as other leashed dogs, unfamiliar people, cats, and cars.

Tip: Require your Cavalier to sit in front of you before getting the tidbit. This prevents the annoying habit some dogs have of dancing around just beyond your reach.

Down: When you need your Cavalier to stay in one place for a long time it is best for it to be left in a Down/Stay. Begin teaching the Down command with the dog in the sitting position. Command "Savannah, down," then show her a tidbit and move it below her nose toward the ground. If she reaches down to get it, give it to her. Repeat, requiring her to reach farther down (without lifting her rear from the ground) until she has to lower her elbows to the ground. Never

Make coming fun (and tasty)!

try to cram your dog into the down position, which can scare a submissive dog and cause a dominant dog to resist. Practice the Down/Stay just as you did the Sit/Stay.

Tip: Occasionally require your dog to lie in a Down/Stay on its side and groom or examine it. Give it a treat for remaining calm. This is a useful exercise for grooming or veterinary attention. You can even teach a separate command ("Side") that means "lie on your side" rather than in the traditional "sphinx" position.

Heel: Your pup should already be acquainted with a lightweight leash at least by the time it has learned "Come." Still, walking alongside of you on lead is a new experience for a youngster, and many will freeze in their tracks once they discover their freedom is being violated. In this case do not simply drag the pup along, but coax it with food. When the puppy follows you, praise and reward. In this way the pup comes to realize that following you while walking on lead pays off.

Some Cavs have a tendency to forge ahead, pulling their hapless

Don't jerk your dog into heel position. Guide it with food and the solid leash. Proper heel position is on your left side, with the dog's neck in line with your leg.

owners behind them, zigzagging from bush to fencepost. Although at times this may be acceptable to you, at other times it will be annoying and perhaps even dangerous. Even if you have no intention of teaching a perfect competition "Heel," you need to teach Heel as a way of letting your Cavalier know it is your turn to be the leader.

Tip: A leash that comes from several feet overhead has virtually no guiding ability whatsoever. You need a lower pivot point for the leash in relation to the dog, and you can achieve this by what is called a "solid leash." This is simply a hollow lightweight tube, such as PVC pipe, about three feet (1 m) long, through which you string your leash. To prevent your

dog from sitting or lying down, loop part of your regular leash around its belly and hold onto that part, so you have a convenient "handle."

Using the solid leash, have your Cavalier sit in Heel position; that is, on your left side with its neck next to and parallel with your leg. Say "Savannah, heel" and step off with your left foot first (remember that you stepped off on your right foot when you left your dog on a Stay; if you are consistent, the foot that moves first will provide an eye-level cue for your little dog). During your first few practice sessions you will keep her on a short lead, holding her in Heel position, and of course praising her. The traditional method of letting the dog lunge to the end of the lead and then snapping it back is unfair if you haven't shown the dog what is expected of it at first. Instead, after a few sessions of showing the dog the Heel position, give her a little more loose lead and use a tidbit to guide her into correct position. If your Cav still forges ahead after you have shown it what is expected, pull it back to position with a quick gentle tug, then release, of the lead. If, after a few days of practice, your dog still seems oblivious to your efforts, then turn unexpectedly several times; teach your dog that it is its responsibility to keep an eye on you.

Tip: Keep up a pace that requires your Cavalier to walk fairly briskly; too slow a pace gives dogs time to sniff, look all around, and in general become distracted; a brisk pace will focus the dog's attention upon you and will generally aid training.

As you progress you will want to add some right, left, and about-faces, and walk at many different speeds. Then practice in different areas (still always on lead) and around different distractions. You can teach your Cav to sit every time you stop. Vary your routine to com-

Your Cavalier will be more comfortable and more likely to stay if you teach it a separate command meaning to lie on its side.

bat boredom, and keep training sessions short. Be sure to give the "OK" command before allowing your dog to sniff, forge, and meander on lead.

The Cavalier Good Citizen

In order to formally recognize dogs that behave in public, the AKC offers the Canine Good Citizen (CGC) certificate. To earn this title your Cavalier must pass the following exercises:
• Accept a friendly stranger who greets you.
• Sit politely for petting by a stranger.
• Allow a stranger to pet and groom it.
• Walk politely on a loose lead.

• Walk through a crowd on a lead.
• Sit and lie down on command and stay in place while on a 20-foot (6.6 m) line.
• Calm down after play.
• React politely to another dog.
• React calmly to distractions.
• Remain calm when tied for three minutes in the owner's absence, under supervision by a stranger.

The CGC is perhaps the most important title your Cavalier can earn. The most magnificent champion in the show or obedience ring is no credit to its breed if it is not a good public citizen in the real world.

Meals Fit for a King

Big puppy dog eyes plead for a bite of your meal. Who could refuse? But those sad eyes are at once the Cavalier's most powerful weapon and own worst enemy. True, dog cannot live by chow alone (according to Cavaliers, at least), but too many snacks given "just this once" will turn your little lapdog into a big fat dog. An occasional snack will not harm most dogs, but the problem with giving snacks to a small dog is that all but the smallest morsels take up what little room it has in its stomach for essential nutritious food.

"You are what you eat" is just as true for dogs as it is for people. Because your Cavalier can't go shopping for its dinner, it "will be what you feed it," so you have total responsibility for feeding your dog a high-quality balanced diet that will enable it to live a long and active life. Choosing a dog food is one of the most confusing yet important decisions a dog owner must make.

Cavalier Cuisine

Although dogs are members of the order Carnivora (meat-eating mammals), they are actually omnivorous, meaning their nutritional needs can be met by a diet derived from both animals and plants. Most dogs do have a decided preference for meat over nonmeat foods, but a balanced meal will combine both meat and plant-based nutrients.

The Choices

Dry food (containing about 10 percent moisture) is the most popular, economical, and healthful, but least palatable form of dog food.

Semimoist foods (with about 30 percent moisture) contain high levels of sugar used as preservatives. Although palatable, convenient, and very handy for traveling, they are not a very good choice for a full diet. They hasten dental plaque accumulation. Pay no attention to their meatlike shapes; they all start out as a powder and are formed to look like meat chunks or ground beef.

Canned foods have a high moisture content (about 75 percent), which helps to make them tasty, but it also makes them comparatively expensive, since you are in essence buying water. A steady diet of canned food would not provide the chewing necessary to maintain dental health. In addition, a high meat content tends to increase levels of dental plaque.

Supplementation with chew sticks, nylon bones, and dog biscuits can provide the necessary chewing action. Dog biscuits provide excellent chewing action, and some of the better varieties provide complete nutrition.

Although a diet of only dry food is preferable from a health standpoint, most people prefer to mix dry food with canned food, adding an occasional semimoist food or dog biscuit for a snack. But beware the tendency to let your dog overindulge; such snacks can lead to fat Cavs.

The Association of American Feed Control Officials (AAFCO) has recommended minimal nutrient levels for dogs based upon controlled feeding studies. Unless you are a nutritionist, the chances of your cooking up a homemade diet that meets these exacting standards are remote. So the first rule is to select a food that states on the label not only that it meets the requirements set by the AAFCO, but also has been tested in feeding trials. You should also realize that when you add table scraps and other enticements, you are disrupting the balance of the diet.

Feed the freshest high-quality food from a name-brand company. Avoid cheap foods, or bizarre foods from unknown companies. Avoid food that has been sitting on the shelf for long periods, or that has holes in the bag or grease that has seeped through the bag.

Find a food that your Cavalier enjoys. Mealtime is a highlight of a dog's day; although a dog will eventually eat even the most unsavory of dog foods if given no choice, it hardly seems fair to deprive your family member of one of life's simple pleasures, and for a dog, one of the most important.

A word of caution: Dogs will often seem to prefer a new food when first offered, but this may simply be because of its novelty. Only after you buy a six-month supply of this alleged Cavalier caviar will you discover it was just a passing fancy. This is one more reason you should never buy a lot of dog food at once.

What's in Dog Food?

When comparing food labels, keep in mind that differences in moisture content make it difficult to make direct comparisons among the guaranteed analyses in different forms of food. The components that vary most from one brand of food to another are protein and fat percentages.

Protein provides the necessary building blocks for growth and maintenance of bones, muscle, and coat, and in the production of infection-fighting antibodies. Meat-derived protein is more highly digestible than plant-derived protein, and is of higher quality. The quality of protein is as important as the quantity of protein.

Puppies and adolescents need particularly high protein levels in their diets, which is one reason they must be fed a food formulated for their life stage. Older dogs, especially those with kidney problems, should be fed lower levels of very high-quality protein. Studies have shown that high protein diets do not cause kidney failure in older dogs; but given a dog in which kidney stress or decompensation exists, a high protein diet will do a lot of harm. If your Cavalier is active throughout the day, or is underweight, you may want to feed it a higher protein food. Most house dogs will do fine on regular adult foods having protein levels of about 20 percent (dry food percentage).

Fat is the calorie-rich component of foods, and most dogs prefer the taste of foods with higher fat content. Fat is necessary to good health, aiding in the transport of important vitamins and providing energy. Dogs deficient in fat often have sparse, dry coats. A higher fat content is usually found in puppy foods. Many high protein foods also have a high fat content. Obese dogs or dogs with heart problems should be fed a lower fat food.

Choose a food that has a protein and fat content best suited for your dog's life stage, adjusting for any weight or health problems; prescription diets formulated for specific health problems are available. Also examine the list of ingredients: a good rule of thumb is that three or four of the first six ingredients should be animal-derived. These tend to be more palatable and more highly digestible than plant-based ingredients; more highly digestible foods mean less stool volume and fewer gas problems.

You may have to do a little experimenting to find just the right food, but

You will help form your puppy into the adult it will become by your selection of its diet. Flowers are not on the menu!

ends can pierce the stomach or intestinal walls.
• Any bone that could be swallowed whole. This could cause choking or intestinal blockage.
• Any cooked bone. Cooked bones tend to break and splinter.
• Raw meat; this could contain salmonella.
• Mineral supplements, unless advised to do so by your veterinarian.
• Chocolate; this contains theobromine, which is poisonous to dogs.
• Alcohol. Small dogs can drink fatal amounts quickly.

Feast or Famine

The dog's wild ancestor, the wolf, evolved to survive feast and famine, gorging following a kill, but then perhaps waiting several days before another feast. In today's world, dogs can feast daily, and without the period of famine, can easily become obese.

Very young puppies should be fed three or four times a day, on a regular schedule. Feed them as much as they care to eat in about 15 minutes. From the age of three to six months, pups should be fed three times daily, and after that, twice daily. Adult dogs can be fed once a day, but it is actually preferable to feed smaller meals twice a day.

Some people let the dog decide when to eat by leaving food available at all times. If you choose to let the dog "self-feed," monitor its weight to be sure it is not overindulging. Leave only dry food for "self-feeding." Canned food spoils rapidly and becomes both unsavory and unhealthful. If your dog overeats, you will have to intervene before you have a chubby Charlie on your hands.

The Fatted Cav

A Cavalier in proper weight should have ribs that can just be felt when you run your hands along the rib

a word of warning: One of the great mysteries of life is why a species, such as the dog, that is renowned for its iron stomach and preference to eat out of garbage cans, can at the same time develop violently upset stomachs simply from changing from one high-quality dog food to another. But it happens. So when changing foods you should do so gradually, mixing in progressively more and more of the new food each day for several days.

What You Should Never Feed

• Bones of chicken, pork, lamb, or fish. If bones are swallowed, their sharp cage. Viewed from above, it should have an hourglass figure. There should be no roll of fat over the withers or rump.

If your Cavalier is overweight, switch to one of the commercially available high-fiber, low-fat and medium-protein diet dog foods, which supply about 15 percent fewer calories per pound. Read the label carefully; many so-called "lite diets" aren't light at all! Make sure family members aren't sneaking the dog forbidden tidbits.

Many people find that one of the pleasures of dog ownership is sharing a special treat with their pet. Rather than giving up this bonding activity, substitute a low-calorie alternative such as rice cakes or carrots. Keep the dog out of the kitchen or dining area at food preparation or mealtimes. Schedule a walk immediately following your dinner to get your dog's mind off your leftovers; it will be good for both of you.

If your dog remains overweight, seek your veterinarian's opinion. Heart disease and some endocrine disorders, such as hypothyroidism or Cushing's disease, or the early stages of diabetes can cause the appearance of obesity and should be ruled out or treated. A potbelly on a lean body is usually a sign of disease, not overeating. However, most cases of obesity are simply from eating more calories than are expended. Obesity predisposes dogs to joint injuries and heart problems.

If you have an underweight dog, try feeding puppy food; add water, milk, bouillon, or canned food and heat slightly to increase aroma and palatability. Milk will cause many dogs to have diarrhea, so try only a little bit at first. Try a couple of dog food brands, but if your choosy Charlie still won't eat then you may have to employ some tough love. Many picky eaters are created when their owners begin to spice up their food with especially tasty treats. The dog then refuses to eat unless the preferred treat is offered, and finally learns that if it refuses even that proffered treat, another even tastier enticement will be offered. Give your dog a good, tasty meal, but don't succumb to puppy dog blackmail or you may be a slave to your Cav's gastronomical whims for years to come.

Your veterinarian should examine your dog if its appetite fails to pick up, or if it still simply can't gain weight. Even more worrisome would be a dog that suddenly lost its appetite or weight. Such a problem can be a warning sign of a physical disorder.

A sick dog, or recuperating dog may have to be coaxed into eating. Cat food or meat baby food are both relished by dogs and may entice a dog without an appetite to eat.

Most Cavaliers are "easy-keepers," meaning they eat readily, are not finicky, and also seem to maintain their weight at an optimal level.

The Cavalier Coiffure

The Cavalier requires only a short grooming session every few days. Grooming is every bit as important for the Cavalier that strolls around the house as it is for the one that struts around the show ring. After all, neither you nor your guests will feel inclined to caress a dog that reeks of "eau de dirty dog." You have in your home two powerful weapons with which to keep your Cavalier's coat fragrant and tangle-free. They are a bathtub and a hairbrush.

The Royal Robes

The most important ingredient in Cavalier grooming is cleanliness. The natural oils of the coat tend to deposit themselves with time, gradually attracting dirt. Dirt and oil are key ingredients in matting. Larger bits of debris, such as leaves and twigs, become focal points around which the coat can wrap,

This king among dogs loses much of its majesty if its royal robes are not regularly groomed.

and can often be found at the core of a mat. When a full-coated Cavalier comes in from the yard, take the time to brush any leaves and twigs from its coat before they become embedded.

Another key ingredient in mat formation is friction. Some friction, such as that between the elbow and chest, is unavoidable, but other friction can be caused by the dog's scratching and chewing itself, perhaps in response to fleas. A Cavalier with fleas is a coat and skin disaster in the making. Use a flea comb to monitor your Cav for the little bloodsuckers. At the same time check the mat-prone areas (the base of the ears as well as between the elbows and chest in heavily coated dogs) for early tangling.

Cavalier coats vary in texture and length. Spayed and neutered dogs tend to have more profuse coats with a fluffier texture. Males tend to have heavier coats. Some dogs have more curl in their coats. The curlier, thicker, and fluffier coats tend to mat more easily. For these coats daily grooming may be needed. Use a slicker brush to remove as much undercoat as possible. Although the Cavalier standard states that no trimming should be done, if you find yourself overwhelmed by a heavy coat in a dog you don't plan to show, you may wish to consult a groomer about trimming or thinning.

The bottoms of the footpads should be trimmed on all dogs. Otherwise the long hair can cause the dog to lose traction and slip on slick floors. Even excessive hair growth on the top of the foot can cause slipping if the dog constantly steps on it. This hair also can act as a magnet for dirt and briars, and when damp, can track considerable mud into the house. Again, although the standard is adamant about no trimming, if you don't plan to show your Cavalier, you may wish to trim the foot hair for both safety and maintenance reasons.

Don't wait until mats have formed to decide something must be done about that coat. Grooming an adult or older puppy that has not been taught how to behave when being groomed is miserable for both of you. Start with a young pup, one too young to form any tangles or mats. Wait until after the youngster has played and is ready to relax. Use a soft brush all over its body, taking care not to hurt the pup and to make brushing a pleasurable experience. You can brush the pup as it lies on your lap or beside you. A grooming table is not really necessary unless you plan to show your Cavalier.

As the pup grows older, its coat will bloom and you will need more heavy-duty grooming tools. A pin brush is usually the instrument of choice, supplemented with a wide-toothed comb and the slicker brush (a brush with many bent teeth.) The choice of brush will depend upon your particular dog's coat type. A more fluffy "cotton" coat will be better tamed by a slicker brush, while a silkier coat will be kept under control with a pin brush. A slicker brush tends to pull more coat out, so if you are trying to nurture every strand, a pin brush is a better choice.

One of the most important brushing tools is actually a spritzer bottle filled with water. Always mist the coat slightly before brushing. This will prevent static electricity from building up, keeping the coat more manageable and less tangle-prone. It will also save the coat by preventing coat breakage while brushing.

Shedding light on shedding: Shedding is induced not by exposure

Tools of the trade.

to warmer temperatures, but by exposure to longer periods of light. This is why indoor dogs, which are exposed to artificial light, tend to shed somewhat all year. Shedding is also under

Trim the hair that protrudes from the bottom of the footpads. The hair growing from the top of the foot should only be trimmed in non-show Cavaliers, and then only if it collects dirt or is so long that it causes the dog to slip.

The Cavalier coat varies in texture and length, but all dogs need the best of nutrition and grooming for their coats to reach their full potential.

hormonal control. After each estrus or litter, the female will undergo a large-scale shedding process.

Splitting hairs: When you do come across a tangle or mat, put those scissors away! First get your dog comfortable, and then carefully pull the mat away from the surrounding hair. A light misting of conditioner can help, or working cornstarch into the mat can make it easier to tease apart. Next try to split the mat in half along its long axis, so you now have two smaller mats. Try

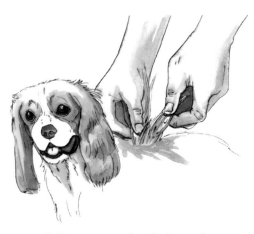

Pull a mat apart along its long axis.

combing out a little of the mat near its tip, holding the mat near the base with your other hand so you aren't pulling the dog's skin. Then repeat the splitting process, so your original big mat is now four little mats. Continue to alternate combing out the ends and resplitting. In severe cases, you may need to give your dog a time break. Either work on other areas of the dog and then return to the mat at the end of your session, or take a full-fledged play break—as long as you don't forget to finish the job you've started!

If you must use scissors, use them to cut the mat along the same axis along which you would be pulling it apart. Wriggle a comb between the mat and the dog's skin to make sure you don't accidentally cut the dog.

There are two reasons you don't want to just snip the mat out in one chunk. The most obvious is that you are snipping away hair that took a long time to grow, and your dog will look scraggly if you continue to cut away. The less obvious is that as the shorter hairs grow back, they tend to weave themselves back into the longer surrounding hair, so that the area is more likely to then mat over and over.

Bathing beauties: The two most important rules about bathing are to do it often enough so that the oil and dirt don't create tangles and mats, and never to bathe a dog with any tangles and mats. Bathing a tangle will have the effect of shrinking the hair on itself, creating a mat that will never be brushed free.

You will generally get better results with a shampoo made for dogs. Dog skin has a pH of 7.5, while human skin has a pH of 5.5; bathing in a shampoo formulated for the pH of human skin can lead to scaling and irritation. Most shampoos will kill fleas even if not especially formulated as a flea shampoo, but none has any residual killing action on fleas, so in general, flea shampoos are not a good buy. No Cavalier owner should be without one of the shampoos that requires no water or rinsing. These are wonderful for puppies, spot-baths, emergencies, and bathing when time does not permit.

A creme rinse applied to the coat after the bath will cause it to be silkier and more manageable. A silky coat could be rendered too limp and flat by a creme rinse, but a cottony, puffy coat would have better shape and manageability. Creme rinses formulated for dogs are ideal, but you can also use a human creme rinse.

Therapeutic shampoos for various skin problems

• dry scaly skin: moisturizing shampoos
• excessive scale and dandruff: anti-seborrheic shampoos, often containing tar and sulfur
• damaged skin: antimicrobials
• itchy skin: oatmeal based anti-pruritics
• bacterial infections: chlorhexidine shampoos

A sink with a hand-held spray makes a handy bathtub. Hold the sprayer against the dog's skin and the dog will not be bothered as much as it would if the spray came from a distance. Use water of a temperature that would be comfortable for you to bathe in, and be sure to keep some running on your own hand to monitor any temperature changes. A fractious puppy could inadvertently hit a faucet knob and cause itself to be scalded. If you keep one hand on your dog's neck or ear, it is less likely to splatter you with a wet dog shake.

Wet your Cavalier down, working forward from the rear. Once the dog is soaked, use your hand to work in the shampoo; it will go a lot farther and be easier to apply if you first mix the shampoo with warm water. Pay special attention to the oily area around the ear base, but avoid getting water

Pay special attention to the face, taking care to avoid eye stain by cleaning below the eyes on a regular basis.

in the dog's ears (try plugging with cotton). Also be careful around the eyes. You can protect them by first putting an ophthalmic ointment in them. Rinse thoroughly, this time working from the head back. A secret of good grooming is to remove every little bubble of shampoo from the coat.

Apply creme rinse sparingly. Work it in gently, taking care not to scrub the coat. As you gain experience with your individual dog, you will learn which areas profit from a little more creme rinse and which can be virtually ignored. You need not rinse the creme rinse out of the coat as thoroughly as you rinsed the shampoo. In fact, some brands of creme rinse can be left in the coat with no rinsing at all, and will continue to discourage tangling. Experiment with different brands; you don't want one that will leave the hair oily, simply silky.

Brush the hair in layers, starting at the bottom. Take care to brush all the way down to the skin.

Drying out: Squeeze the excess water from your dog's coat, then wrap a towel around it and carry it to a waterproof room where it can shake until the room is soaked.

Blow dry a thin coat while combing the hair backwards for more body. Blow dry a thick coat through a mesh or stocking to train it to lie flat.

The best way to dry your Cavalier is with a blow-dryer, brushing the coat from the skin out as the warm air blows upon it. Use warm or even cool air. Hot air can burn the dog's skin, as well as damage the coat. A blow-dryer with a stand is the easiest to use. Blow-dry and brush the dog using the same brushing technique as you do in your normal grooming session.

If your Cavalier's coat is thin, brush the hair backwards as you dry it, so that it tends to stand away from the body. If your Cavalier's coat tends to be thick and wavy, you can blow it dry through a mesh that will hold the coat close to the body. Try placing an old stocking (with the foot cut out and holes cut for the dog's legs) over the dog's body. First brush the wet hair straight.

Accustoming your young Cavalier to a blow-dryer can be challenging at first. Start with the dryer away from the head, on a low setting. It helps if it's a cold day and your dog can come to appreciate the warmth of the dryer.

If you can't blow your dog dry you can wrap a towel around it to soak up as much moisture as possible. Keep the dog in a warm room and change the towel often. Finally, if the weather is warm you can let the dog sun dry, but beware: after all that work your nice clean Cav is apt to try to dry itself by rolling in the dirt!

Quick Fixes
• Wet or muddy feet can be dried and cleaned by sprinkling a liberal amount of cornstarch into the hair and then brushing it out. You may have to repeat the application a few times.
• Pine tar can be loosened with hair spray.
• Other tar can be worked out with vegetable oil followed by dishwashing detergent.
• Chewing gum can be eased out by first applying ice.
• Skunk odor can be partially washed

away with tomato juice. First shampoo, then leave juice on for 15 minutes.

Battle of the Bugs

Fleas and ticks will quickly undo any good all your grooming efforts have accomplished, besides subjecting your dog to many health problems and considerable discomfort. Fleas can carry tapeworms, and ticks can carry Rocky Mountain spotted fever, tick paralysis, Lyme disease, babesiosis, and most commonly, "tick fever" (erlichiosis), all potentially fatal diseases.

Look for fleas and their evidence around the chest, belly, genital areas, and especially, the base of the tail. Fleas leave behind a black pepper-like substance (actually flea feces) that turns red upon getting wet. Ticks can be found anywhere on the dog, but most often burrow around the ears, neck, chest, and between the toes.

No flea zone: Recent advances in flea and tick control have finally put dog owners on the winning side. In any but the mildest of infestations, these new products are well worth their initial higher purchase price. Consider carefully the correct choice of products for your dog and situation:
• lufenuron (marketed under the brand name Program) is given as a pill once a month. Fleas that bite the dog and ingest the lufenuron in the dog's system are rendered sterile. It is extremely safe. All animals in the environment must be treated in order for the regime to be effective, however. Some owners give this product rave reviews, while others have seen little improvement. The latter probably are in situations in which they are being constantly reinfested from untreated animals.
• imidacloprid (marketed under the brand name Advantage) is a liquid applied once a month on the animal's back. It gradually distributes itself over the entire skin surface and kills at least 98 percent of the fleas on the animal within 24 hours. It is not absorbed into the dog's body, yet it can continue to kill fleas for one month. Exposure to rain won't hinder its effectiveness, but it will not withstand swimming or bathing. Thus, this product may not be the ideal choice if you intend to stay on a weekly bathing schedule.
• fipronil (marketed under the brand name Frontline) comes as either a spray that you must apply all over the dog's body, or as a self-distributing liquid applied only on the dog's back. Once applied, fipronil collects in the hair follicles and then wicks out over time. Thus, it is resistant to being washed off and can kill fleas for up to three months on dogs. It is also effective on ticks for a shorter period.
• pyriproxyfen (marketed under the brand names Nylar, Sumilar, and others) is an insect growth regulator available as an animal or premise spray. It is marketed in different strengths and formulations, and it can protect in the home or yard for six to twelve months, and on the animal for 100 days, depending upon the particular product.

Traditional flea control products are either less effective or less safe than these newer products. The permethrins and pyrethrins are safe, but have virtually no residual action. The large family of cholinesterase inhibitors (Dursban, Diazinon, malathion, Sevin, Carbaryl, Pro-Spot, Spotton) last a little longer, but have been known to kill dogs when overused, used in combination with cholinesterase-inhibiting yard products, or with cholinesterase-inhibiting dewormers. Incidentally, the ultrasonic flea-repelling collars have been shown to be both ineffective on fleas and irritating to dogs. Scientific studies have also shown that feeding dogs brewer's yeast or garlic, as has been advocated for years by many dog owners, is ineffective against fleas. However, many owners swear it works and it certainly does no harm.

It is gratifying to share your home with a clean, parasite-free dog.

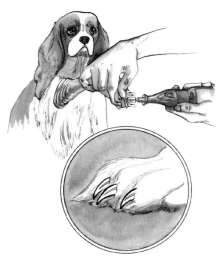

Cut the nails as close to the "quick" as possible. If you elect to use a nail grinder, place the dog's foot in an old stocking, and push each nail through so that the long hair of the feet doesn't get caught in the grinder.

Ticked off: To remove a tick, use a tissue or tweezers, since some diseases can be transmitted to humans. Grasp the tick as close to the skin as possible, and pull slowly and steadily, trying not to leave the head in the dog. Clean the site with alcohol. Often a bump will remain after the tick is removed, even if you got the head. It will go away with time. Don't ever try to burn a tick out! You may set fire to your dog.

Beauty Is Skin Deep

Skin problems in all dogs are the most common problems seen by veterinarians, and the most common of all skin problems is flea allergy dermatitis (FAD). Itchy, crusted bumps with hair loss in the region around the rump, especially at the base of the tail, results from a flea bite anywhere on the dog's body.

Besides FAD, dogs can have allergic reactions to pollens, house dust mites, or other inhaled allergens. Food allergies can also occur.

Pyoderma, with pus-filled bumps and crusting, is another common skin disease. Impetigo is characterized by such bumps and crusting most often in the groin area of puppies. Both are treated with antibiotics and antibacterial shampoos.

In seborrhea, there may be excessive dandruff or greasiness, often with excessive ear wax and rancid odor. Treatment is with antiseborrheic shampoos.

The Hidden Bear Claws

The long hair of the feet may hide the toenails, causing many owners to neglect cutting the nails as often as needed. When you can hear the pitter-patter of clicking nails, that means that with every step the nails are hitting the floor, and when this happens the bones of the foot are spread, causing discomfort and eventually splayed feet

By introducing your pup to water slowly and kindly, you will create an adult that will not object to bathtime.

and lameness. If dew claws are left untrimmed they can get caught on things more easily or actually loop around and grow into the dog's leg. You must prevent this by trimming your dog's nails every week or two.

Begin by handling the feet and nails daily, and then cutting the very tips of your puppy's nails every week, taking special care not to cut the "quick" (the central core of blood vessels and nerve endings). You may find it easiest to cut the nails with your Cavalier lying on its back in your lap. If you look at the bottoms of the nails you will see a solid core culminating in a hollowed nail. Cut the tip up to the core, but not beyond. On occasion you will slip up and cause the nail to bleed. This is best stopped by styptic powder, but if this is not available dip the nail in flour or hold it to a wet tea bag.

Taking the Bite Out of Dental Bills

Plaque and tartar are not only unsightly, but contribute to bad breath and health problems. Dry food and hard dog biscuits, rawhide and nylabone chewies are helpful, but not totally effective at removing plaque. Brushing your Cav's teeth once or

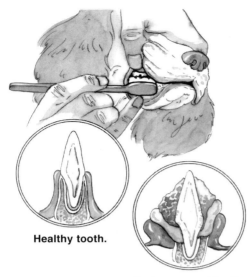

Healthy tooth.

Tartar-covered tooth with infected gum.

Brushing your dog's teeth will prevent costly dental procedures and disease. Left unattended, teeth can become seriously infected.

twice weekly (optimally daily) with a child's toothbrush and doggy toothpaste is the best plaque remover. If not removed, plaque will attract bacteria and minerals, which will harden into tartar. If you cannot brush, your veterinarian can supply cleansing solution that will help to kill plaque-forming bacteria. You may have to

have your veterinarian clean your dog's teeth as often as once a year.

Neglected plaque and tartar can cause infections to form along the gum line. The infection can gradually work its way down the sides of the tooth until the entire root is undermined. The tissues and bone around the tooth erode, and the tooth finally falls out. Meanwhile, the bacteria may have entered the bloodstream and been carried throughout the body, causing infection in the kidneys and heart valves. In fact, periodontal disease is a leading cause of heart valve disease in dogs. Neglecting your dog's teeth can do more harm than causing bad breath; it could possibly kill your dog.

Between four and seven months of age, Cavalier puppies will begin to shed their baby teeth and show off new permanent teeth. Often deciduous (baby) teeth, especially the canines (fangs), are not shed, so that the permanent tooth grows in beside the baby tooth. If this condition persists for over a week, consult your veterinarian. Retained baby teeth can cause misalignment of adult teeth. Correct occlusion (bite) is important for good dental health. In a correct Cavalier bite, the top incisors should fit snugly in front of the bottom incisors. Too large a gap between the upper and lower incisors could cause eating difficulties or result in the tongue lolling out of the mouth.

Long Live the King!

Dogs today can live longer and healthier lives thanks to many advances in veterinary medicine. But all the advances in the world won't do your dog a bit of good unless you know how to do your part. Your Cavalier can tell you where it hurts if you only know how to listen to it. You listen by means of a weekly health check and a regular veterinary checkup.

The Health Check

A weekly health check should be part of your grooming procedure. Examine the following:
• the eyes for discharge, cloudiness, or discolored "whites"
• the ears for foul odor, redness, or discharge
• the mouth for red, bleeding, or swollen gums, loose teeth, ulcers of the tongue or gums, or bad breath
• the nose for thickened or colored discharge
• the skin for parasites, hair loss, crusts, red spots, or lumps
• the feet for cuts, abrasions, split nails, bumps, or misaligned toes

Observe your dog for signs of lameness or incoordination, a sore neck, circling, loss of muscling, and for any behavioral change. Run your hands over the muscles and bones and check that they are symmetrical from one side to the other. Weigh your dog and observe whether it is putting on fat or wasting away. Check for any growths or swellings, which could indicate cancer or a number of less serious problems. A sore that does not heal or any pigmented lump that begins to grow or bleed should be checked by a veterinarian immedi-

ately. Look out for mammary masses, changes in testicle size, discharge from the vulva or penis, increased or decreased urination, foul-smelling or strangely colored urine, incontinence, swollen abdomen, black or bloody stool, change in appetite or water consumption, difficult breathing, lethargy, gagging, or loss of balance.

To take your dog's temperature, lubricate a rectal thermometer (preferably the digital type) and insert it about two inches (5 cm), and leave it for about one minute. Do not allow your dog to sit down on the thermometer! Normal temperature for a Cavalier is around 101°F (38°C), ranging from 100 to 102.5°F (37.7–39.2°C). Call your veterinarian at once if the temperature is over 104°F (40°C).

To check the pulse press the femoral artery, located inside the rear leg, where the thigh meets the abdomen. Normal pulse rates range from 80 to 140 beats per minute in an awake Cavalier.

The Health Team

Your health check can go only so far in ensuring your pet's healthy status. A good veterinarian will also be needed to monitor your dog's internal signs by way of blood tests and other procedures.

When choosing your veterinarian, consider availability, emergency arrangements, costs, facilities, and ability to communicate. Some veterinarians will include more sophisticated tests as part of their regular checkups. Such tests, while often desirable, will add to the cost of a visit. Unless money is no object, reach an understanding about procedures and fees

Your puppy will depend on you for proper health care in order to share a long life with you.

be appreciative if your Cav is clean, parasite-free, and under control during the examination.

Be Prepared

Because there are no paramedics for dogs, you must assume the role of paramedic and ambulance driver in case of an emergency. Now is the time to prepare for these lifesaving roles. Study the emergency procedures described in this chapter, and keep this guide handy. Misplaced instructions can result in the loss of critical time. Know the phone number and location of the emergency veterinarian in your area. Keep the number next to the phone; don't rely on your memory during an emergency situation. Always keep enough fuel in your car to make it to the emergency clinic without stopping for gas. Finally, stay calm. It will help you help your dog, and will help your dog stay calm as well. A calm dog is less likely to go into shock.

Even experienced dog owners have a difficult time deciding what constitutes a true emergency; when in doubt, err on the side of caution and call the emergency clinic or your veterinarian for an opinion.

You should maintain a medical kit for your Cavalier, with these items:
• rectal thermometer
• scissors
• tweezers
• sterile gauze dressings
• self-adhesive bandage (such as Vet-Wrap)
• instant cold compress
• antidiarrhea medication
• ophthalmic ointment
• soap
• antiseptic skin ointment
• hydrogen peroxide
• clean sponge
• pen light
• syringe
• towel

before having them performed. You and your veterinarian will form a team who will work together to protect your Cavalier's health, so your rapport with your veterinarian is very important. Your veterinarian should listen to your observations and should explain to you exactly what is happening with your dog. The clinic should be clean and have safe, sanitary overnight accommodations. After-hour emergency arrangements should be made clear.

When you take your Cavalier to the veterinary clinic, don't let it mingle with or frighten other animals, who may be sick. If you think your dog may have a contagious illness, inform the clinic beforehand so that you can use a secondary entrance. Your veterinarian will

Poisoning

Symptoms and treatment vary depending on the specific poison. In most cases, home treatment is not advisable. If in doubt about whether poison was ingested, call the vet anyway. If possible, bring the poison and its container to the veterinarian.

Two of the most common and life-threatening poisons eaten by dogs are Warfarin (rodent poison) and especially, ethylene glycol (antifreeze). Veterinary treatment must be obtained within two to four hours of ingestion of even tiny amounts if the dog's life is to be saved.

Signs: vary with the poison; commonly include vomiting, convulsions, staggering, and collapse.

Treatment: Check the label on the container (if available) for directions. Call the vet or poison control hotline; give as much information as possible. Induce vomiting (except in cases outlined below) by giving either hydrogen peroxide (mixed 1:1 with water), salt water, or dry mustard and water. Treat for shock and get to the vet at once. Be prepared for convulsions or respiratory distress.

Do not induce vomiting if 1) the poison was an acid, alkali, petroleum product, solvent, cleaner, tranquilizer; 2) a sharp object was swallowed; 3) the dog is severely depressed, convulsing, or comatose; 4) over two hours have passed since ingestion. If the dog is not convulsing or unconscious: dilute the poison by giving milk, vegetable oil, or egg whites. Activated charcoal can adsorb many toxins. Baking soda or milk of magnesia can be given for ingested acids, and vinegar or lemon juice for ingested alkalis.

Don't flirt with disaster. Do not let your puppy mingle with other dogs until it is vaccinated.

- stethoscope (optional)
- oxygen (optional)
- first aid instructions
- veterinarian and emergency clinic numbers
- poison control center number

Move an injured dog carefully, preferably on a hard board. Use a blanket or towel if a board is not available.

61

When Confronted with an Emergency

• Make sure breathing passages are open. Remove any collar and check the mouth and throat.
• Move the dog as little and as gently as possible.
• Control any bleeding.
• Check breathing, pulse, and consciousness.
• Check for signs of shock (very pale gums, weakness, unresponsiveness, faint pulse, shivering). Keep the dog warm and calm.
• Never use force; do nothing to cause extreme discomfort.
• Never remove an impaled object unless it is blocking the airway.

An Ounce of Prevention

The best preventive medicine is that which prevents accidents: a well-trained dog in a securely fenced yard or on a leash, and a properly dog-proofed home. Other preventive steps must be taken to avoid diseases and parasites, however.

Vaccinations: Rabies, distemper, leptospirosis, canine hepatitis, parvovirus, and corona virus are highly contagious and deadly diseases that have broken many a loving owner's heart in the past. Now that vaccinations are available for these maladies one would think they would no longer be a threat, but many dogs remain unvaccinated and continue to contract and spread these potentially fatal illnesses. Don't let your little Cavalier be one of them.

Vaccinations are also available for kennel cough and Lyme disease, but may be optional depending upon your dog's lifestyle. In fact, in most parts of the country, the possibility of complications due to the Lyme vaccine are greater than the probability of problems due to actually contracting Lyme disease. Your veterinarian can advise you. Always make sure your dog is in good health at the time it is vaccinated. Many dogs seem to feel under the weather for a day or so after getting their vaccinations, so don't schedule your appointment the day before boarding, a trip, or a big doggy event.

Puppies receive their dam's immunity through nursing in the first days of life. This is why it is important that your pup's mother be properly immunized before breeding, and that your pup be able to nurse from its dam. The immunity gained from the mother will wear off after several weeks, and then the pup will be susceptible to disease unless you provide immunity through vaccinations. The problem is that there is no way to know exactly when this passive immunity will wear off, and vaccinations given before that time are ineffective. You must therefore revaccinate over a period of weeks so that your pup will not be unprotected and will receive effective immunity.

Your pup's breeder will have given the first vaccinations to your pup before it was old enough to go home with you. Bring all information about your pup's vaccination history to your veterinarian on your first visit so that

Sample Vaccination Schedule

Age (weeks)	Vaccine
6–8	distemper + hepatitis + parainfluenza + parvovirus
10–12	distemper + hepatitis + parainfluenza + parvovirus + leptospirosis
14–16	distemper + hepatitis + parainfluenza + parvovirus + leptospirosis, rabies
18–20	distemper + hepatitis + parainfluenza + parvovirus + leptospirosis

the pup's vaccination schedule can be maintained. Meanwhile, it is best not to let your pup mingle with strange dogs.

Neuter or Spay Your Pet Today

Another veterinary procedure that can save your pet's life is early spaying or neutering. If you don't intend to breed your pet—and there are more good reasons not to breed than to breed (see page 80)—plan to schedule this simple surgery before your pet reaches puberty, at least by eight or nine months of age. Not only will you avoid contributing to pet overpopulation, but you will help safeguard your Cavalier's life.

• Spaying (surgical removal of ovaries and uterus) before the first estrus drastically reduces the chances of breast or uterine cancer.
• Castration (surgical removal of the testicles) virtually eliminates the chance of testicular or prostate cancer.
• Dogs with undescended testicles have an increased risk of testicular cancer, and should be castrated before three to five years of age.
• In a recent study, 80 percent of all dogs killed by automobiles were intact (unneutered) males, apparently making their rounds.

Internal Parasite Control

Internal parasites can rob your dog of vital nutrients, good health, and sometimes, even a long life. The most common internal parasites set up housekeeping in the intestines and heart.

Intestinal parasites: Hookworms, whipworms, and ascarids are types of nematode parasites that can infect dogs of all ages, but have their most devastating effect on puppies. When you take the pup to be vaccinated bring along a stool specimen so that your veterinarian can also check for these parasites. Even pups from the most fastidious breeders often have

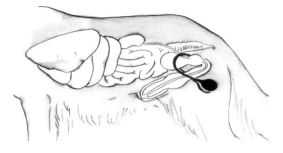

Male internal organs. The testicles (shown in black) are removed in castration.

worms at some point. This is because some types of larval worms become encysted in the dam's body long before she ever became pregnant; perhaps when she herself was a pup. Here they lie dormant and immune from worming, until hormonal changes due to her pregnancy cause them to be activated, and then they infect her fetuses or her newborns through her

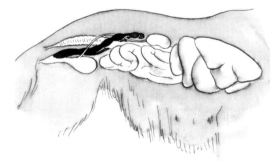

Female internal organs. The ovary and uterus (shown in black) are removed in spaying.

Sudden lethargy can be a sign that your Cavalier is sick.

those available through your veterinarian. Left untreated, worms can cause vomiting, diarrhea, dull coat, listlessness, anemia, and death. Some worms can be passed on to humans, especially children. Have your puppy tested for internal parasites regularly. Some heartworm preventives also prevent most types of intestinal worms (but not tapeworms).

Tapeworms (cestodes) tend to plague some dogs throughout their lives. There is no preventive, except to diligently rid your Cavalier of fleas, because fleas transmit tapeworms to dogs. Tapeworms look like moving white flat worms on fresh stools, or may dry up and look like rice grains around the dog's anus. Tapeworms are one of the least debilitating worms, but their segments can be irritating to the dog's anal region, and are certainly unsightly.

Dog owners tend to have some strange ideas concerning "worms." Let a dog scoot its rear on the ground, and its owner automatically diagnoses it as "wormy." Although scooting may be a sign of tapeworms, a dog that repeatedly scoots more likely has impacted anal sacs. Somebody somewhere popularized the notion that if you feed a dog sugar and sweets it will get worms. There are good reasons not to feed a dog sweets, but worms have nothing to do with them. And some companies have made a fortune at the expense of dog owners and their dogs by promoting the idea that dogs should be regularly wormed every month or so. Dogs should be wormed only when they have been diagnosed with worms. No worm medication is completely without risk, and it is foolish to use it carelessly.

Heartworms: Heartworms are a deadly nematode parasite carried by mosquitoes. Wherever mosquitoes are present, dogs should be on heartworm prevention. Several effective types of

milk. You may be tempted to pick up some worm medication and worm your puppy yourself. Don't. Over-the-counter wormers are largely ineffective and often more dangerous than

The life-cycle of the tapeworm. Note that a flea is a necessary intermediate host.

heartworm preventive are available, with some also preventing many other types of worms. Some require daily administration, while others require only monthly administration. The latter type are more popular and actually have a wider margin of safety and protection. They don't stay in the dog's system for a month, but instead act on a particular stage in the heartworm's development. Giving the drug each month prevents any heartworms from ever maturing. In warm areas your dog may need to be on prevention year-round, but in milder climates your dog may need to be on prevention only during the warmer months. Consult with your veterinarian about the heartworm situation in your area and when your puppy should begin taking the preventive.

If you forget to give the medicine as prescribed, your dog may get heartworms. A dog with suspected heartworms should not be given the daily preventive because a fatal reaction could occur. The most common way of checking for heartworms is to check the blood for circulating microfilarae (the immature form of heartworms), but this method may fail to detect the presence of adult heartworms in as many as 20 percent of all tested dogs. An "occult" heartworm test, though slightly more expensive, tests for the presence of antigens to heartworms in the blood, and is more accurate. With either test, the presence of heartworms will not be detectable until nearly seven months after infection. Heartworms are treatable in their early stages, but the treatment is expensive and not without risks (although a less risky treatment has recently become available). If untreated, heartworms can kill your pet.

Protozoa: Puppies and dogs also suffer from protozoan parasites, such as coccidia and especially, Giardia. These can cause chronic or intermit-

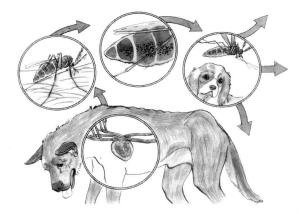

Life-cycle of heartworms. When a mosquito bites an infected dog, it ingests circulating immature heartworms, which it then pass on to the next dog it bites.

tent diarrhea, and can be diagnosed with a stool specimen.

Medications

When giving pills, open your dog's mouth and place the pill well to the back and in the middle of the tongue. Close the mouth and gently stroke the throat until your dog swallows. Prewetting capsules or covering them with cream cheese or some other food helps prevent capsules from sticking to the tongue or roof of the mouth. For liquid medicine, tilt the head back, keep the dog's mouth almost (but not quite tightly) closed and place the liquid in the pouch of the cheek. Then hold the mouth closed until the dog swallows. Always give the full course of medications prescribed by your veterinarian. Don't give your dog human medications unless you have been directed to do so by your veterinarian. Some medications for humans have no effect upon dogs, and some can have a very detrimental effect.

HOW-TO:
First Aid Procedures

Cool a dog with heatstroke by covering it with wet towels and placing it in front of a fan, or placing the dog in cool water. Dunking the dog in ice water is dangerous because it constricts peripheral blood vessels.

For the following situations, initiate first aid and then transport to the veterinarian (call first).

Heatstroke
Signs: Rapid, loud breathing; abundant thick saliva, bright red mucous membranes, high rectal temperature. Later signs: unsteadiness, diarrhea, coma.

Treatment: Wet the dog down and place it in front of a fan or immerse the dog in cool water. Do not plunge the dog into ice water. Offer small amounts of water for drinking. You must lower your dog's temperature quickly, but not below 100°F (37.7°C).

Breathing Difficulties
Signs: gasping for breath with head extended, anxiety, weakness; advances to unconsciousness, bluish tongue (Exception: carbon monoxide poisoning causes bright red tongue).

Treatment: If not breathing:
1. Open dog's mouth, clear passage of secretions and foreign bodies.
2. Pull dog's tongue forward.
3. Seal your mouth over dog's nose and mouth, blow gently into dog's nose for three seconds, then release.
4. Continue until dog breathes on its own.
• In case of **drowning**, turn dog upside down, holding around its waist, so water can run out of its mouth. Then administer

mouth-to-nose respiration, with the dog's head positioned lower than its lungs.
• For obstructions, wrap your hands around the abdomen, behind the rib cage, and compress briskly. Repeat if needed. If the dog loses consciousness, extend the head and neck forward, pull the tongue out fully, and explore the throat for any foreign objects.

Hypothermia
Signs: Shivering, cold feeling, sluggishness.

Treatment: Warm gradually. Wrap in blanket. Place plastic bottles filled with hot water outside the blankets (not touching the dog). You can also place a plastic tarp over the blanket, making sure the dog's head is not covered. Monitor temperature.

Convulsions or Seizures
Signs: drooling, stiffness, muscle spasms

Treatment: Wrap the dog securely in a blanket to prevent it from injuring itself on furniture or stairs. Remove other dogs from the area (they may attack

the convulsing dog). Never put your hands (or anything) in a convulsing dog's mouth. Treat for shock. Make note of all characteristics and sequences of seizure to help diagnose the cause.

Hypoglycemia (low blood sugar)
Signs: Appears disoriented, weak, staggering. May appear blind, and muscles may twitch. Later stages lead to convulsions, coma, and death.

Treatment: Give food, or honey or syrup mixed with warm water.

Open Wounds
Signs: Wounds are an emergency if there is profuse bleeding, if extremely deep, if open to chest cavity, abdominal cavity, or head.

Treatment: Control massive bleeding first. Cover the wound with clean dressing and apply pressure; apply more dressings over the others until bleeding stops. Also elevate wound site, and apply cold pack to site. If an extremity, apply pressure to the closest pressure point as follows:

• For a front leg: inside of front leg just above the elbow
• For a rear leg: inside of thigh where the femoral artery crosses the thigh-bone
• For the tail: underside of tail close to where it joins the body.

Use a tourniquet only in life-threatening situations and when all other attempts have failed. Check for signs of shock.

Sucking chest wounds: Place plastic or other nonporous sheet over the hole and bandage it to make an airtight seal.

Abdominal wounds: Place warm wet sterile dressing over any protruding internal organs; cover with bandage or towel. Do not attempt to push organs back.

Head wounds: Apply gentle pressure to control bleeding. Monitor for loss of consciousness or shock and treat accordingly.

Electrical shock

Signs: Collapse, burns inside mouth

Treatment: Before touching dog, disconnect plug or cut power; if that cannot be done immediately, use a wooden pencil, spoon, or broom handle to knock cord away from dog. Keep dog warm and treat for shock. Monitor breathing and heartbeat.

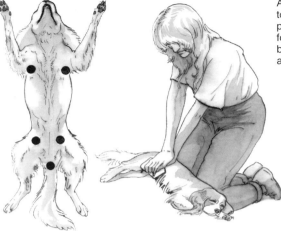

Apply pressure to the closest pressure point for uncontrolled bleeding of an extremity.

Poisonous Snakebites

Signs: Swelling, skin discoloration, pain, fangmarks, restlessness, nausea, weakness

Treatment: Restrain the dog and keep it quiet. Be able to describe the snake. Only if you can't get to the vet, apply a pressure bandage between the wound and the heart tight enough to slow blood returning to the heart.

Deep Burns

Signs: Charred or pearly white skin; deeper layers of tissue exposed.

Treatment: Cool burned area with cool packs, towels soaked in ice water, or by immersing in cold water. If over 50 percent of the dog is burned, do not immerse as this increases likelihood of shock. Cover with clean bandage or towel to avoid contamination. Do not apply pressure; do not apply ointments. Monitor for shock.

Situations not in this list can usually be treated with the same first aid as for humans. In all cases, the best advice is to consult a veterinarian.

Understanding Mitral Valve Disease

Cavalier King Charles Spaniels have one devastating hereditary disease: mitral valve disease (MVD). The canine heart consists of four chambers and four one-way valves. The two upper chambers are the left and right atria (singular: atrium), which function as receiving areas for blood returning to the heart. The two lower chambers are the left and right ventricles, which pump the blood out of the heart and throughout the body. The mitral valve controls the flow of blood from the left atrium to the left ventricle.

When the left ventricle contracts, the mitral valve is forced shut, and the blood is pushed through the aorta into the circulatory system. In MVD, the folds of tissue that make up the sides of the mitral valve shrivel and curl, so that the valve no longer closes tightly during the contraction of the left ventricle. The gap in the valve allows the blood to flow backward into the atrium when the left ventricle contracts, a condition termed mitral regurgitation (MR). Because blood flows back into the atrium, the flow to the rest of the body is decreased. The left atrium increases in size in order to accommodate the increased blood volume, and the left ventricle increases in size in order to pump more blood in an attempt to compensate for the decreased blood flow to the rest of the body. As the condition worsens, the left side of the heart becomes increasingly enlarged, and symptoms of congestive heart failure may become evident. Fluid may accumulate in the lungs because of the high pressure in the left atrium causing blood and fluid to back up into the capillaries of the lungs. This fluid accumulation, along with bronchial compression from the enlarged heart, leads to coughing.

Symptoms: In some dogs, few outward symptoms are present, despite increasing deterioration of cardiac function. The first sign to be noted is usually exercise intolerance, but this often goes unnoticed in house pets. Coughing is often the first symptom that owners detect. Labored or increased rates of breathing may also be present. As the disease progresses, dogs may collapse or faint due to insufficient blood flow to the brain. Symptoms may worsen rapidly, or may progress gradually over a period of years.

Diagnostic tests: Preliminary diagnosis of MVD can usually be made by listening to the heart. With a stethoscope, mitral regurgitation can be detected as a murmur. An electrocardiogram (ECG) can monitor the beats of the heart and record how aberrant they are. The pattern of irregularities can point to problems in different areas of the heart. Many veterinarians can perform an ECG in their office by transmitting the signals to a veterinary hospital specializing in cardiology.

1. Pulmonary artery (to lung)
2. Pulmonary vein (from lung)
3. Aorta
4. Left atrium
5. Mitral valve
6. Left ventricle
7. Left side of heart
8. Right side of heart
9. Right ventricle
10. Right atrium
11. Vein from body
12. Vein from head

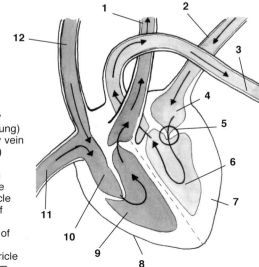

The flow of blood as it is pumped through a healthy heart.

Radiographs (X rays) can show whether the heart is enlarged. These can also be done by your local veterinarian. More advanced procedures such as two-dimensional echocardiography and Doppler echocardiography can further aid in determining severity, but are best performed by a cardiologist. This would usually entail going to a veterinary teaching hospital.

Treatment: Unfortunately, there is no cure or prevention for MVD. Cavalier owners should be especially diligent in preventing periodontal disease, which can cause valvular disease in any dog. Even so, good dental hygiene cannot prevent MVD. The disease gets progressively worse, although the rate of deterioration varies widely. Some affected dogs can still live long lives. Obese dogs should be put on a diet. Low-sodium diets may be helpful, but their treatment value has not been proved. They are of no value in preventing MVD. Although the progression of the disease cannot be slowed through current means, drugs can help alleviate some of the symptoms. Drug therapies may include diuretics (to reduce fluid accumulation), vasodilators (to expand blood vessels), and possibly some other drugs.

If your veterinarian is not aware of the most current research findings about MVD in Cavaliers, ask to be referred to a cardiologist at the nearest veterinary teaching university.

Why Cavaliers? Hereditary problems can become widespread in a breed through several mechanisms. One such mechanism is the "founder effect," in which most members of the breed descend from one or a few initial foundation stock, and unfortunately, one or more of those founding fathers (or mothers) carried the defective gene. When the breeding pool is small, closely related individuals must be interbred, increasing the likelihood that recessive deleterious genes will be paired in the resulting offspring.

Today's Cavaliers all descend from six dogs. Unfortunately, at least one of them probably carried genes that resulted in mitral valve disease. When their descendants were interbred, some of the unlucky ones received a combination of genes that resulted in the faulty valves. When the breed was still relatively rare, nobody recognized that there was a breed-related problem. But during the 1970s boom in popularity in Great Britain, it began to be apparent that heart problems were occurring in Cavaliers at a greater rate and at a younger age than in most other breeds.

Incidence: A survey undertaken in the early 1980s found that by five years of age 50 percent of Cavaliers had mitral regurgitation. Not only did the percentage of affected dogs continue to increase with age, but the severity of

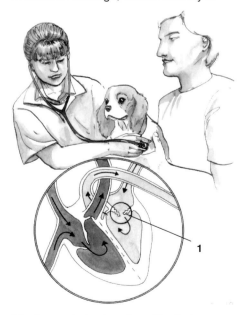

Mitral regurgitation in a dog with mitral valve degeneration.

1. Mitral valve

the regurgitation increased with time. An early 1990s study in the United States also found over 50 percent of Cavaliers aged four or more to have mitral regurgitation. The percentage of affected dogs and the severity of the disease both increased when the dogs were rechecked one year later.

An early 1990s Swedish study found that a pet health insurance company processed claims related to heart disease in Cavaliers at a rate 14 times the mean rate for all other breeds. Claims related to euthanasia or death in Cavaliers aged seven to ten years were processed 13 times more than in other breeds.

As in many other breeds affected by MR, males seem to be more often and more severely affected than females. MR is seen in several other small breeds, but in no other breed is it as common, nor manifested at such an early age, as it is in the Cavalier.

Breeding guidelines: A 1996 Swedish study demonstrated that parents with valvular disease are more likely to produce offspring with valvular disease. However, the disease did not seem to be inherited in a simple dominant-recessive mode. Instead, it seems to be polygenic in nature, meaning that it depends upon the interplay of many gene pairs. When a sufficient number of deleterious gene pairs are present, they exceed a threshold, and the disease manifests itself in the individual.

The early manifestation of the disease is a mixed blessing. For the owner of the affected dog, it is a terrible heartache. But for the future of the breed, it may be the saving grace. In many breeds disease occurs at an age after dogs have been bred. In Cavaliers, however, the early incidence means that there is time to insure that dogs are clear before breeding them. The current practice of breeding young dogs that have been checked free of murmurs has not lowered the incidence of the disease. Therefore, researchers suggest that Cavaliers should never be bred before the age of five, at which time they should be checked and certified free of murmurs. Information on the relatives of all potential breeding stock should be gathered, including information on the age at which the dog was last checked clear of murmurs, or the age at which a murmur was first detected, the intensity of the murmur, and the age of death. Dogs with a higher incidence of affected relatives should not be bred.

In Great Britain, a program has been developed in which dogs are examined every year by a veterinarian, who then completes a certificate describing the findings. The results are sent to the breed club. Breeders are encouraged to participate in the program, and to breed only dogs that have been certified clear—and the older, the better.

The future: Anybody unfortunate enough to have their beloved Cavalier die from MVD knows too well the grief and frustration of losing a pet too early to a disease for which there was no prevention and no cure. Exciting discoveries are being made in the area of canine genetics, though, and perhaps the genes causing MVD will eventually be isolated. This has happened for several canine diseases, so that dogs can be screened for the presence of the gene by a simple test almost at birth. The polygenic nature of MVD will make this a far more difficult search, however.

Unfortunately, funding for such research is scarce. Several organizations fund research into canine disease, most notably the AKC Canine Health Project and the Morris Animal Foundation. You can do your part by contacting these organizations or the Cavalier club and donating toward Cavalier MVD research.

Symptoms of Common Health Problems

Coughing: Allergies, foreign bodies, pneumonia, parasites, tracheal collapse, tumors, and especially, kennel cough and heart disease, can all cause coughing.

Kennel cough is a highly communicable airborne disease caused by several different infectious agents. It is characterized by a gagging cough arising eight days after exposure. Inoculations are available and are an especially good idea if you plan to have your dog around other dogs at training classes or while being boarded.

Heart disease can result in coughing, most often following exercise or in the evening. See Understanding Mitral Valve Disease (page 68) for a description of this all too common problem of the Cavalier.

Any persistent cough should be checked by your veterinarian. Coughing irritates the throat and can lead to secondary infections if allowed to continue unchecked. It can also be miserable for the dog.

Vomiting: Vomiting is a common occurrence that may or may not indicate a serious problem. Vomiting after eating grass is common and usually of no great concern. Overeating is a common cause of occasional vomiting in puppies, especially if they follow eating with playing. Feed smaller meals more frequently if this becomes a problem. Vomiting immediately after meals could indicate an obstruction of the esophagus. Repeated vomiting could indicate that the dog has eaten spoiled food, undigestible objects, or may have stomach illness. Veterinary advice should be sought. Meanwhile withhold food (or feed as directed for diarrhea) and restrict water.

Consult your veterinarian immediately if your dog vomits a foul substance resembling fecal matter (indicating a blockage in the intestinal tract), blood (partially digested blood resembles coffee grounds), or if there is projectile or continued vomiting. Sporadic vomiting with poor appetite and generally poor condition could indicate internal parasites or a more serious internal disease that should also be checked by your veterinarian.

Diarrhea: Diarrhea can result from overexcitement or nervousness, a change in diet or water, sensitivity to certain foods, overeating, intestinal parasites, viral or bacterial infections, or ingestion of toxic substances. Bloody diarrhea, diarrhea with vomiting, fever, or other signs of toxicity, or a diarrhea that lasts for more than a day should not be allowed to continue without veterinary advice. Some of these symptoms could indicate potentially fatal disorders.

Less severe diarrhea can be treated at home by withholding or severely restricting food and water for 24 hours. Ice cubes can be given to satisfy thirst. Administer Pepto-Bismol in the same weight dosage as recommended for humans. A bland diet consisting of rice, tapioca, or cooked macaroni, along with cottage cheese or tofu for protein, should be given for several days. Feed nothing else. The intestinal tract needs time off in order to heal.

Urinary tract diseases: If your dog has difficulty or pain in urination, urinates suddenly and often but in small amounts, or passes cloudy or bloody urine, it may be suffering from a problem of the bladder, urethra, or prostate. Dribbling of urine during sleep indicates a hormonal problem. Urinalysis and a rectal exam by your veterinarian are necessary to diagnose the exact nature of the problem. Bladder infections must be treated promptly to prevent the infection from reaching the kidneys.

Kidney disease, ultimately leading to kidney failure, is one of the most common ailments of older dogs. The earliest symptom is usually increased urination. Although the excessive urination may cause problems in keeping your house clean or your night's sleep intact, never try to restrict water from a dog with kidney disease. Increased urination can also be a sign of diabetes or a urinary tract infection. Your veterinarian can discover the cause with some simple tests, and each of these conditions can be treated. For kidney disease, a low-protein and low-sodium diet can slow the progression.

In males, infections of the prostate gland can lead to repeated urinary tract infections, and sometimes painful defecation or blood and pus in the urine. Castration and long-term antibiotic therapy is required for improvement.

Impacted anal sacs: Constant licking of the anus or scooting of the anus along the ground are characteristic signs of anal sac impaction. Dogs have two anal sacs that are normally emptied by rectal pressure during defecation. Their musky-smelling contents may also be forcibly ejected when a dog is extremely frightened. Sometimes the sacs fail to empty properly and become impacted or infected. This is more common in small dogs, obese dogs, dogs with seborrhea, and dogs that seldom have firm stools. Impacted sacs cause extreme discomfort and can become infected. Treatment consists of manually emptying the sacs and administering antibiotics. As a last resort, the sacs may be removed surgically.

Endocrine disorders: The most widespread hormone-related disorders in the dog are diabetes, hypothyroidism, and Cushing's syndrome. The most common of these, hypothyroidism, also has the least obvious symptoms, which may include weight gain, lethargy, and coat problems such as oiliness, dullness, symmetrical hair loss, and hair that is easily pulled out.

The hallmark of diabetes is increased drinking and urination, and sometimes increased appetite with weight loss.

Cushing's syndrome (hyperadrenocorticism) is seen mostly in older dogs, and is characterized by increased drinking and urination, potbellied appearance, symmetrical hair loss on the body, darkened skin, and susceptibility to infections.

All these conditions can be diagnosed with simple tests, and can be treated with drugs by your veterinarian.

Limping

Limping may or may not indicate a serious problem. Mild lameness should be treated by complete rest; if it still persists after three days, your dog will need to be examined by its veterinarian. When associated with extreme pain, fever, swelling, deformity, or grinding or popping sounds, you should have your veterinarian examine your Cavalier at once. Ice packs may help minimize swelling if applied immediately after an injury. Avoid pain medications that might encourage the use of an injured limb.

Fractures should be immobilized by splinting above and below the site of fracture before moving the dog (a rolled magazine can work well on legs in an emergency). Immediate veterinary attention is required.

Knee injuries, especially of the cruciate ligaments, are common in dogs; most do not get well on their own. Cruciate surgery requires a commitment to careful nursing and should not be undertaken casually.

Puppies are especially susceptible to bone and joint injuries, and should never be allowed to jump from high places or run until exhausted. Persistent limping in puppies may result from one of several developmental bone problems, and should be checked by the veterinarian. Both puppies and adults should be discouraged from romping on slippery floors that could cause them to lose their footing.

In older dogs, or dogs with a previous injury, limping is often the result of osteoarthritis. Arthritis can be treated with aspirin, but should be done so only under veterinary supervision. Do not use naxopren. Any time a young or middle-aged dog shows signs of arthritis, especially in a joint that has not been previously injured, it should be examined by its veterinarian.

Patellar luxation is the bane of many small breeds, including, to some extent, the Cavalier. In most dogs the patella (kneecap) is held in its proper position by a deep groove, but if the groove is too shallow (or if the tibia is misaligned) the patella can pop out of place. When out of place, the knee cannot be straightened and the dog will hold the leg up, usually only for a few steps at a time, but sometimes for extended periods. When standing, the leg may appear bowed either in or out. Patellar luxation can be corrected surgically, the sooner the better. The longer the surgery is postponed, especially in a growing puppy, the greater the chance the leg will be permanently deformed. Patellar luxation is also discussed on page 15.

Canine hip dysplasia (CHD) is also seen in Cavaliers. The head of the femur bone does not fit snugly into the socket of the pelvis, so that the hip joint is lax. In severe cases it develops early in life and is characterized by reluctance to exercise or climb steps, abnormal gait, and atrophy of the thigh muscles. More commonly, CHD appears later in life and symptoms are less severe. This chronic form is characterized by less severe pain or exercise intolerance, and sometimes stiffness of gait. CHD results as an interplay of genetic and environmental factors. Unfortunately, despite a good

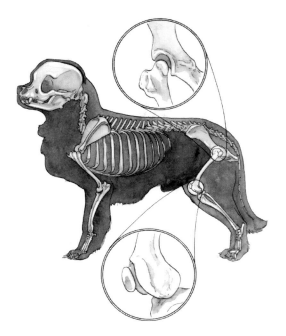

The Cavalier skeleton. In patellar luxation, the kneecap (patella) often pops out of its proper position. In hip dysplasia, the head of the thigh bone (femur) does not fit snugly into the pelvic socket.

deal of research, the exact cause of CHD remains unknown.

CHD will eventually cause arthritic changes. In severe cases, surgery may be advisable. Talk to your veterinarian about the options available, and consider consulting with a veterinary orthopedist at a veterinary teaching university. CHD is also discussed on page 15.

Bites and stings: Dogs bite dogs. The problem with dog (or any animal) bites is that they are prone to infection. If your dog is bitten, allow some bleeding, then clean the area thoroughly and apply antibiotic ointment. It's best not to suture most animal bites, but a large one (over one-half inch [1.2 cm] in diameter), or one on the face or other prominent position may need to be sutured. A course of oral antibiotics will probably be necessary. Of course, with any animal bite, rabies is a concern.

Dogs are often stung by insects on the face or feet. Remove any visible stingers as quickly as possible. Administer baking soda and water paste to bee stings, and vinegar to wasp stings. Clean the area and apply antibacterial ointment. Keep an eye on the dog in case it has an allergic reaction, including swelling that could interfere with breathing, change in consciousness, restlessness, vomiting, diarrhea, seizures, or collapse. If so, seek immediate veterinary attention.

Eye problems: Those big brown eyes come with a price tag: their fairly large size makes them slightly more vulnerable to corneal scratches. Squinting or tearing can be due to an irritated cornea or foreign body. Examine under the lids and flood the eye with saline solution, or use a moist cotton swab to remove any debris. If no improvement is seen after a day, have your veterinarian take a look. A watery discharge without squinting can be a symptom of allergies or a tear drainage problem. A clogged tear drainage duct can cause the tears to drain onto the face, rather than the normal drainage through the nose. Your veterinarian can diagnose a drainage problem with a simple test.

A thick ropy mucous or crusty discharge suggests conjunctivitis or dry eye (keratoconjunctivitis sicca, or KCS). In KCS there is inadequate tear production, resulting in irritation to the surface of the eye whenever the dog blinks. The surface of the eye may appear dull. KCS can cause secondary bacterial infection or corneal ulcers. In fact, KCS should be suspected in any dog in which recurrent corneal ulceration or conjunctivitis is a problem. In past years KCS was treated with the frequent application of artificial tears, which most owners found difficult to dispense as often as needed. Recent drug advances treat the causes of KCS with ophthalmic immunosuppressive therapy. This therapy can be quite effective if begun early.

As your Cavalier ages it is natural that the lens of the eye becomes a little hazy. You will notice this as a slightly grayish appearance behind the pupils. But if this occurs at a young age, or if the lens looks white or opaque, ask your veterinarian to check your dog for cataracts. In cataracts the lens becomes so opaque that light can no longer reach the retina; as in humans, the lens can be surgically replaced with an artificial lens. Hereditary cataracts have been reported in Cavaliers.

If an eye is injured, cover it with clean gauze soaked in water or saline solution. For contact with irritants, flush for five minutes with water.

Any time your dog's pupils do not react to light or when one eye reacts differently from the other, consult the veterinarian immediately. These symptoms could indicate a serious ocular or neurological problem.

The eyes are such complex and sensitive organs that you should always err on the side of caution. Seek veterinary attention at the slightest sign of a problem.

Ear care: The dog's ear canal is made up of an initial long vertical segment that then abruptly angles to run horizontally toward the skull. This configuration provides a moist environment in which various ear infections can flourish. Add to this the Cavalier's hanging ear flap, and you have the recipe for an ear problem, especially when the ears are covered with thick, heavy hair. At the same time, the Cavalier is not as prone to ear problems as are breeds in which the hair grows down into the ear canal. It is fairly simple to keep the Cavalier's ears healthy by checking them regularly and not allowing moisture or debris to build up in them.

Signs of ear problems include inflammation, discharge, debris, foul odor, pain, scratching, shaking, tilting of the head, or circling to one side. Extreme pain may indicate a ruptured eardrum. Ear problems can be difficult to cure once they have become established, so early veterinary attention is crucial. Bacterial and fungal infections, ear mites or ticks, foreign bodies, inhalant allergies, seborrhea, or hypothyroidism are possible underlying problems. Grass awns are one of the most common causes of ear problems in dogs that spend time outdoors. Keep the ear lubricated with mineral oil, and seek veterinary treatment as soon as possible. Problems only get worse.

When treating the ears with drops or liquids, you will have to wash the hair under the ear almost every day, or the oily liquid that is shaken from the ears will stick in the hair and can cause matting. Use a no-rinse shampoo and be careful not to get water or shampoo into the ear canal.

Don't stick cotton swabs into the ear canal; they can irritate the skin and pack debris into the horizontal canal. Never use powders in the ear, which can cake, or hydrogen peroxide, which leaves the ear moist.

Ear mites, often found in puppies, are highly contagious and intensely irritating. An affected dog will shake its head, scratch its ears, and carry its head sideways. A dark, dry, waxy buildup resembling coffee grounds, usually in the ear canal of both ears, is the ear mite's signature. This material is actually dried blood mixed with ear wax. If you look through a magnifying glass at some of this wax on a piece of dark paper, you should be able to see the tiny white moving culprits. Over-the-counter ear mite preparations can

The dog's ear canal consists of an initial vertical canal, with an abrupt curve leading to a horizontal canal. In a dog with hanging ear flaps, moisture can become trapped in the horizontal canal, providing a perfect environment for infections.

cause worse irritation; ear mites are best treated by your veterinarian.

If you must treat the dog yourself, get a pyrethrin/mineral oil ear product. First flush the ear with an ear-cleaning solution. You can buy a solution from your veterinarian, or make a mixture of one part alcohol to two parts white vinegar. Cleaning solutions will flush debris but will not kill mites or cure infections. Then apply the ear mite drops daily for at least a week, and possibly a month. Because these mites are also found in the dog's fur all over its body, you should also bathe the pet weekly with a pyrethrin-based shampoo, or apply a pyrethrin flea dip, powder, or spray. Separate a dog with ear mites from other pets and

Dogs with thick hair on their ears require extra vigilance in ear care.

Keep an eye out for eye problems that could affect those big brown eyes.

wash your hands after handling its ears. Ideally, every pet in a household should be treated.

Many people automatically assume any ear problem is due to ear mites, but unless you actually see mites, don't treat the dog for them. You could make another problem worse.

The smelly dog: Doggy odor is not only offensive; it is unnatural. Don't exile the dog, or hold your breath. If a bath doesn't produce results, it's time to use your nose to sniff out the source of the problem. Infection is a common cause of bad odor; check the mouth, ears, feet, and genitals. Generalized bad odor can indicate a skin problem, such as seborrhea. Don't ignore bad odor, and don't make your dog take the blame for something you need to fix.

Strange Behavior

Fly-catching behavior is considered to be a form of hallucinatory or epileptic behavior in which the dog snaps repeatedly in the air, as though trying to catch flying insects that are not there. It usually first appears between eight months and one and a half years of age. Consult your veterinarian if the episodes increase in frequency or magnitude. New treatments for epilepsy may be effective in controlling the behavior.

Episodic weakness or collapse are as yet unexplained behaviors that have been reported in some Cavaliers after exercise. The affected dogs walk with a stiff gait, head down and rump up, and then fall over without losing consciousness. The cause is not yet known, but it is believed to have a hereditary component.

To a Ripe Old Age

The Cavalier's perpetual puppy persona and look sometimes mislead owners into forgetting that Cavaliers, like all dogs, get old. One day you will look at your Cavalier and be shocked to discover its face has silvered and its gait has stiffened. It sleeps longer and more soundly than it did as a youngster, and is slower to get going. It may be less eager to play and more content to lie in the sun. Though you might feel sad, be mindful that getting your dog to healthy old age is a worthy accomplishment. Just make sure that you appreciate all the stages along the way.

The Older Cavalier

It is important to keep your older dog active. Both physical activity and metabolic rates decrease in older animals, meaning that they require fewer calories to maintain the same weight. Older dogs that continue to be fed the same as when they were young risk becoming obese; such dogs have a greater risk of cardiovascular and joint problems.

Older dogs should be fed several small meals instead of one large meal, and should be fed on time. Moistening dry food or feeding canned food can help a dog with dental problems enjoy its meal.

Although many geriatric dogs are overweight, others lose weight and may need to eat puppy food in order to keep the pounds on. Most older dogs do not require a special diet unless they have a particular medical need for it (e.g. obesity: low calorie; kidney failure: low protein; heart failure: low sodium.)

Arthritis is a common cause of intermittent stiffness and lameness. A soft warm bed combined with moderate activity can help, and your veterinarian can prescribe drugs for severe cases.

Older dogs tend to have a stronger body odor, but don't just ignore increased odors. They could indicate specific problems, such as periodontal disease, impacted anal sacs, seborrhea, ear infections, or even kidney disease. Any strong odor should be checked by your veterinarian. Like people, dogs lose skin moisture as they age, and though dogs don't have to worry about wrinkles, their skin can become dry and itchy. Regular brushing can help by stimulating oil production.

The immune system may be less effective in older dogs, so that it is increasingly important to shield your dog from infectious disease, chilling, overheating, and any other stressful conditions.

Older dogs present a somewhat greater anesthesia risk. Most of this increased risk can be negated, however, by first screening dogs with a complete medical work up.

Vomiting and diarrhea in an old dog can signal many different problems; keep in mind that a small older dog cannot tolerate the dehydration that results from continued vomiting or diarrhea and you should not let it continue unchecked. The older dog should see its veterinarian at least twice a year. Blood tests can detect early stages of diseases that can benefit from treatment.

The older Cavalier will tend to take life a little easier.

In general, any ailment that an older dog has is magnified in severity compared to the same symptoms in a younger dog. A long life depends upon good genes, good care, and good luck.

Common Symptoms and Ailments of Older Dogs

• diarrhea: kidney or liver disease, pancreatitis
• coughing: heart disease, tracheal collapse, lung cancer
• difficulty eating: periodontal disease, oral tumors
• decreased appetite: kidney, liver, or heart disease, pancreatitis, cancer
• increased appetite: diabetes, Cushing's Syndrome
• weight loss: heart, liver or kidney disease, diabetes, cancer
• abdominal distension: heart or kidney disease, Cushing's Syndrome, tumor.
• increased urination: diabetes, kidney or liver disease, cystitis, Cushing's Syndrome
• limping: arthritis, patellar luxation
• nasal discharge: tumor, periodontal disease

Some older dogs become cranky and less patient, especially when dealing with puppies or boisterous children. But don't just excuse behavioral changes, especially if sudden, as due simply to aging. They could be symptoms of pain or disease.

Older dogs may experience hearing or visual loss. Be careful not to startle a dog with impaired senses, as a startled dog could snap in self-defense. The slight haziness that appears in the older dog's pupils is normal and has minimal effect upon vision, but some dogs, especially those with diabetes, may develop cataracts. These can be removed by a veterinary ophthalmologist if they are severe. Decreased tear production increases the chances of KCS (dry eye). Dogs with gradual vision loss can cope well as long as they are kept in familiar surroundings and extra safety precautions are followed.

Long trips may be grueling, and boarding in a kennel may be extremely upsetting. Introduction of a puppy or new pet may be welcomed and encourage your older dog to play, but if your dog is not used to other dogs the newcomer will more likely be resented and be an additional source of stress.

If you are lucky enough to have an old Cavalier, you still must accept that an end will come. Heart disease, kidney failure, and cancer eventually claim most of these senior citizens. Early detection can help delay their effects, but unfortunately, can seldom prevent them ultimately.

Farewell to a Friend

Despite the best of care, a time will come when neither you nor your veterinarian can prevent your cherished pet from succumbing to old age or an incurable illness. It seems hard to believe that you will have to say good-bye to someone who has been such a focal point of your life; in truth, a real member of your family. That dogs live such a short time compared to humans is a cruel fact, but one that you must ultimately face.

Try to realize that both of you have been fortunate to have shared so many good times, but make sure that your Cavalier's remaining time is still pleasurable. Many terminal illnesses make your dog feel very ill, and there comes a point where your desire to keep your friend with you as long as possible may not be the kindest thing for either of you. If your dog no longer eats its dinner or treats, this is a sign that it does not feel well and you must face the prospect of doing what is best for your beloved friend.

Euthanasia is a difficult and personal decision that no one wishes to make, and no one can make for you.

Ask your veterinarian if there is a reasonable chance of your dog getting better, and if it is likely that your dog is suffering. Ask yourself if your dog is getting pleasure out of life, and if it enjoys most of its days. Financial considerations can be a factor if it means going into debt in exchange for just a little while longer. Your own emotional state must also be considered.

If you do decide that euthanasia is the kindest farewell gift for your beloved friend, discuss with your veterinarian beforehand what will happen. Euthanasia is painless and involves giving an overdose of an anesthetic. If your dog is scared of the veterinarian clinic, you might feel better having the doctor meet you at home or come out to your car. Although it won't be easy, try to remain with your dog so that its last moments will be filled with your love; otherwise have a friend that your Cavalier knows stay with it. Try to recall the wonderful times you have shared and realize that however painful losing such a once-in-a-lifetime dog is, it is better than never having had such a partner at all.

Many people who regarded their Cavalier as a member of the family nonetheless feel embarrassed at the grief they feel at its loss. Yet this dog has often functioned as a surrogate child, best friend, and confidant. Partnership with a pet can be one of the closest and most stable relationships in many people's lives. Because people are often closer to their pets than they are to distant family members, it is not uncommon to feel more grief at the loss of the pet.

Unfortunately, the support from friends that comes with human loss is too often absent with pet loss. Such well-meaning but ill-informed statements as "he was just a dog" or "just get another one" do little to ease the pain, but the truth is that many people simply don't know how to react and probably aren't really as callous as they might sound. There are, however, many people who share your feelings and there are pet bereavement counselors available at many veterinary schools.

After losing such a cherished friend, many people say they will never get another dog. True, no dog will ever take the place of your dog. But you will find that another Cavalier is a welcome diversion and will help keep you from dwelling on the loss of your first pet, as long as you don't keep comparing the new dog to the old. True also, by getting another dog you are sentencing yourself to the same grief in another 10 to 15 years, but wouldn't you rather have that than miss out on a second once-in-a-lifetime dog?

In Line for the Throne

Everybody loves puppies, and one of the few things cuter than a Cavalier is a Cavalier puppy. Don't get so infatuated by those spaniel eyes that you throw reason to the wind, however. Before you breed your Cavalier, remember that puppies are puppies for a very short time. Think hard before you quadruple your dog family population.

Not So Fast

One of the most unfortunate aspects of dog ownership is the compulsion so many people have to breed a litter. Rarely is this done with enough foresight or responsibility. The result, most often, is a grave disservice to themselves, their pet, the breed, the resulting puppies, and to their new owners. Unless you have studied the breed, have proved your female to be a superior specimen in terms of conformation, health, and temperament, and plan to take responsibility for each and every puppy for the rest of its life, you have no business doing anything but having your dog neutered.

Because Cavaliers are currently an expensive breed to purchase, new owners too often reason that they can make their money back by breeding their Cavalier. For those people who have worked and sacrificed to improve the breed, the high prices charged for their puppies will never come close to compensating them for the long hours of worry and toil. It is terribly unfair for you to waltz in, breed an inferior dog in order to reap some imaginary harvest, and leave the breed worse off. From an ethical viewpoint, a Cavalier should be a true member of your family, one you would no more exploit and breed for money than any other family member. Finally, keep in mind that you probably will not make very much money by breeding your Cavalier. Cavaliers are expensive because they have relatively small litters and they are comparatively rare except in the higher social echelons. The small litters mean that there is very little profit to be made after paying for a stud fee, prenatal care, postnatal care, whelping supplies, puppy food, supplements, toys, advertising, vaccinations, and deworming, not to mention the hours upon hours of cleanup you will be performing for free. As Cavaliers become more popular, there will always be the unethical or uninformed who will breed their pets. Competition

Think before you breed or you may find yourself with too much of a good thing.

will drive prices down, so that, just as has happened with every other rare or expensive breed, they will eventually be cheap as supply exceeds demand.

Keep in mind that breeding is not doing your female any favor. There is definite discomfort and a certain amount of danger to any dog, but especially a small dog, when whelping a litter. Watching a litter be born is not a good way to teach the children the miracle of life; there are too many things that can go wrong. Moreover, a spayed female is less likely to develop breast cancer and a number of other hormone-related diseases (see page 63).

The fact that your Cavalier is purebred and registered does not mean it is breeding quality, any more than the fact that you have a driver's license qualifies you to build race cars. Only 10% of all Cav's have qualities which justify breeding. Serious breeders have spent years researching genetics and the breed; they breed only the best specimens, and they screen for hereditary defects in order to obtain healthy puppies. Unless you have done the same before mating your Cavalier, you are undoing the hard work of those who have dedicated their lives to bettering the breed.

Ethical breeders breed a litter only after studying the breed standard, studying pedigrees, and studying individual dogs to find the most advantageous match of conformation, temperament, and health, then proving the worth of both prospective parents through competitions. They interview prospective buyers and get deposits from them before the breeding even takes place. They have money set aside for prenatal and postnatal care, and emergency funds and vacation time available for whelping or postwhelping complications. They have the commitment to keep every single puppy for the rest of its life should good

Ruby is a solid red.

Blenheim has white markings over a red base.

81

homes not be available or should any ever have to be returned. And they worry a lot. Is it any wonder that some of the best breeders breed the least?

Royal Lineages

If you still have not been dissuaded from breeding your Cavalier, you owe it to yourself and the breed to settle for no less than the best available stud. You will not find this stud advertised in the newspaper. If you are contemplating breeding, you should be familiar with prominent kennels and studs. Look for a stud that is superior in the areas where your bitch needs improvement. Look for an owner who is honest about the stud's faults, health problems, and temperament.

A responsible stud owner will have proved the stud by earning titles, will have complete records and photos of other litters the stud has produced, and will insist that your bitch and her pedigree be compatible before accepting her for breeding.

Although most female Cavaliers will generally have their first estrus between six and nine months of age, they are neither mentally nor physically mature enough to be bred. After all, they are still puppies themselves and should be enjoying their own puppyhoods. In fact, new Cavalier breeding guidelines advocate that both male and female should optimally be about six years of age before breeding, at which time they should be checked to

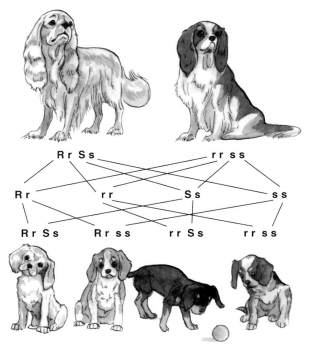

A breeding between a ruby (solid color red) that happens to be carrying recessive parti-color and black and tan genes would have the genotype **Rr Ss.** If this dog were bred with a tricolor (parti-color black and tan—which would have the genotype **rr ss**), all colors would be possible in their offspring.

ensure they are still free of cardiac problems.

Monitor the female closely for signs of "heat" (estrus). These include swelling of the vulva and a red discharge. Most dogs are breedable for several days sometime between the 8th and 18th day of estrus, although earlier and later alliances have been known to result in pregnancy. Your veterinarian can also monitor her progress with vaginal smears or blood tests. As she approaches her receptive stage, she will tend to "flag" her tail, or cock it to the side when the male approaches or if you scratch around the base of her tail. Your best indicator is the stud dog; experienced stud dogs do not need calendars or microscopes!

Predicting Coat Color

Coat color genetics of the Cavalier are relatively simple. A dog can either be solid color or parti-color (that is, white along with a color). Think of the parti-color as a solid-colored dog that had white paint splashed over its body, and you will realize that Cavaliers only come in two "base" colors: red, and black and tan. Blenheim is a parti-color version of red ("ruby"). Tricolor is the parti-color version of black and tan.

Genes at one location determine whether a dog will be either red or black and tan, while genes at a different location determine whether it will be solid or parti-colored. In each case the genes act in a simple dominant/recessive manner. That is, at each location two genes (or alleles) are present, and one allele (the dominant one) can mask the presence of the other (recessive) allele. In the case of Cavaliers, the red (**R**) allele is dominant to the black and tan (**r**) allele, and the solid (**S**) allele is dominant to the parti-color (**s**) allele.

The possible genotypes of the four colors are as follows:

red solid (ruby): **RR SS** or **Rr SS** or **RR Ss** or **Rr Ss**
bl/tan solid (black and tan): **rr SS** or **rr Ss**
red parti (Blenheim): **RR ss** or **Rr ss**
bl/tan parti (tricolor): **rr ss**

For practical purposes this means that the breedings between dogs of the various colors can result in offspring colored as follows. Note that not all breedings will result in as great a variety of colors as listed here, because the diversity will only occur if the parents have hidden recessives.

bl/tan parti X bl/tan parti → bl/tan parti
bl/tan parti X red parti → red parti, bl/tan parti
red parti X red parti → red parti, bl/tan parti
bl/tan solid X bl/tan solid → bl/tan solid, bl/tan parti
bl/tan solid X red solid → all colors
red solid X red solid → all colors
bl/tan solid X bl/tan parti → bl/tan solid, bl/tan parti
bl/tan solid X red parti → all colors
red solid X red parti → all colors

Lady-in-Waiting

Now you have two months to wait and plan. Gradually increase and change the expectant mother's food to a high-quality puppy food as time progresses. Keep her in shape; a well-conditioned dog will have fewer problems whelping. At the end of the first month your veterinarian may be able to feel the developing puppies, but this is not always accurate. Two encouraging signs of pregnancy that might appear at around this same time are a clear mucous discharge from the vagina and enlarged, pink nipples. If at any time the discharge is not clear seek veterinary attention at once.

Avoid letting her run up and down stairs, especially after the first month. When carrying her be sure that you are not putting pressure on her abdomen. Do not give any medication

Black and tan is black with tan points.

Tri-color has white markings over a black and tan base.

without your veterinarian's advice. Your pregnant female should be isolated from strange dogs beginning three weeks before her due date; exposure to certain viruses during that time does not allow her to develop sufficient immunity to pass to her puppies, and can result in the loss of the litter.

Many females are prone to false pregnancies: a condition in which the breasts become slightly enlarged and may even have some milk. Pronounced cases involving large amounts of milk production, weight gain, and even nesting behavior and the adoption of certain toys as "babies" may be unhealthy and should be checked by your veterinarian. Some can be so convincing that even experienced breeders have thought their bitch was in whelp until she failed to deliver puppies!

Labor of Love

If you have never assisted at a small dog whelping, talk to your veterinarian or an experienced Cavalier breeder about what to expect. You should prepare a whelping box that will double as a nursery, and place it in a warm, quiet room. You can use the bottom of a plastic dog cage or a sturdy clean cardboard box. Place the box on a rug or other insulating material, and line the inside with newspaper (preferably blank newsprint, and never colored sections), or better yet, washable towels or blankets. Don't use indoor-outdoor carpeting, which tends to interact with urine in such a way as to irritate pups' skin.

You should be counting the days from the first breeding carefully. While 63 days is the average canine gestation time, there is some variability, with small dogs tending to be somewhat early rather than late. A few days before the due date, clip the hair from the areas around the vulva and the breasts, and then thoroughly wash these areas.

You can get about 12 hours advance notice by charting the expectant mother's temperature starting around the 56th day; when her temperature drops to about 98°F (36.6°C) and remains there, make plans to stay home because labor should begin within 12 hours. Warm the whelping box to 80°F (26.6°C), and prepare for a long night. She will become more restless, refuse to eat, and repeatedly demand to go out. Make her as comfortable as possible and do not let her go outside alone where she might have a puppy.

As labor becomes more intense, she may scratch and bite at her bedding. The puppies are preceded by a water bag; once this has burst the first puppy should be born soon. As each baby is born, watch that the mother clears its face so it can breathe. If she does not, hold the pup to her. If she still ignores it, clear the face yourself and use the nasal aspirator to clear the nostrils. The dam should chew the umbilical cord herself, but if she does not, then you can tie it off about ¾ inch (1.9 cm) from the puppy with dental floss, and then cut it on the side away from the pup. Each puppy should be followed by an afterbirth, which the dam will try to eat. Allow her to eat one as it contains important hormones affecting milk production, but eating too many will give her diarrhea. You must count the placentas to make absolutely sure that none was retained in her; retained placentas can cause serious infection. If a placenta is retained, seek veterinary attention. The dam should lick the puppy to dry and stimulate it, and the pup should begin nursing immediately. If the dam ignores a pup, offer it to her. You may have to dry it yourself and place it on a nipple. You should not try to take over the dam's duties, but monitor her mothering and be ready to step in should she fall short. Most Cavaliers

The new family should be given plenty of privacy.

are easy whelpers and good mothers, but you need to be vigilant just in case.

It is not always easy to tell when the last puppy is born. If you have any doubts, have your veterinarian check her (you should bring her and the puppies for a post-birth check the next day anyway). Typical Cavalier litters have four or five pups, but litters of up to nine have been recorded.

Signs of a possible whelping emergency:
• More than 24 hours have passed since the dam's temperature dropped without the onset of contractions.

The Whelping Kit
· whelping box
· rectal thermometer
· many towels and washcloths
· nasal aspirator
· dull scissors
· dental floss
· heating pad or heat lamp
· bitch's milk replacement
· highlighted whelping instructions
· emergency phone numbers

- More than two hours of intermittent contractions have passed without progressing to hard, forceful contractions.
- More than 30 minutes of strong contractions have passed without producing a puppy.
- More than 15 minutes have passed since part of a puppy protruded through the vulva and the puppy makes no progress.
- Large amounts of blood are passed during whelping. The normal color fluid is dark green to black.

Never allow a dam in trouble to continue unaided. She may need a cesarean to save her life, and the longer it is put off the poorer the chances of survival for her and her puppies.

The Queen Mother

Giving birth to a litter of puppies is grueling and not without danger, but even after a successful whelping, things can go wrong that can threaten the dam and puppies.

Pyometra: It is normal for the dam to have a dark bloody vaginal discharge (called lochia) for a week or two after the birth, but you should bring your dog to the veterinarian's office if there are any signs of infection or foul odor associated with it. If accompanied by fever, it could indicate pyometra, and call for a trip to the emergency veterinarian. In pyometra, the uterus becomes infected and the best treatment is immediate spaying. If left untreated, the dam will die.

Eclampsia: Eclampsia is a life-threatening convulsive condition that may occur in late pregnancy or more commonly, during lactation. It is more prevalent in small breeds and with larger litters. The first signs are nervous panting and restlessness, followed by increasing irritability and disorientation. Muscular twitching, fever, and rapid heart rate are definite danger signals. Convulsions are the last stage before death.

The condition seems to be brought about by a depletion of calcium. Many breeders of small dogs used to supplement with calcium throughout the pregnancy in an attempt to ward off eclampsia, but it is now thought that such supplementation may actually promote eclampsia by interfering with the internal calcium-regulating mechanisms.

Once eclampsia does occur, the bitch must be taken immediately to the veterinarian for an injection of calcium and Vitamin D in order to save her life. Eclampsia is an extreme emergency.

Mastitis: Sometimes the dam's breasts become hard, swollen, or painful, indicating mastitis. Warm compresses can help her feel more comfortable, but if pus and blood are mixed with the milk, you will need to prevent the pups from nursing from those nipples and your veterinarian will probably prescribe antibiotics.

In cases of infections, mastitis, or eclampsia you may have to wean the puppies early. By fitting the mother with a "body suit," such as a wide sweater sleeve with four leg holes, she can stay with the pups without letting them nurse.

The Royal Heirs

Newborn Cavalier pups typically weigh between five and eight ounces (140–224 gm). Pups weighing as little as three ounces (84 gm) have survived, but may need special care. Larger pups, weighing up to 14 ounces (392 gm), have been recorded in very small litters. Such pups may be later to walk than smaller pups, but will eventually be every bit as agile.

You should weigh each puppy on a gram scale daily for the first two weeks to make sure that it is gaining weight. If not, ask your veterinarian about supplemental feeding. Monitor the nursing puppies to make sure they are getting milk. Pups with cleft palates will have milk bubbling out of their nostrils as they attempt to nurse. Consult with your veterinarian for treatment options.

Puppies cannot regulate their body temperature, and chilling can quickly result in death. This is especially critical for small breeds. The dam is understandably reluctant to leave them at first; you should place them in a warm box and encourage the dam to go out to relieve herself on a regular schedule. Maintain the pup's environment at 85 to 90°F (29–32°C) for the first week, 80°F (26.6°C) for the second week, and 75°F (24°C) for the third and fourth weeks. These ambient temperatures can be lowered if a heating pad is available. Place a well-insulated heating pad on one side of the whelping box, so that the pups can crawl on or off it. While you don't want the pups to chill, neither do you want them to become overheated. Never feed a chilled puppy, except for a few drops of sugar water.

Cavalier puppies are born with pink noses and eye rims that gradually turn dark beginning a few days after birth. If you elect to remove dewclaws or to dock the tail, it should be done at about three days of age. Most breeders are leaving the tail intact.

Pups are blind and deaf at birth, but have well-developed senses of touch, taste, and smell. Pups use these senses to locate their dam's mammary glands and crawl to them. The puppies' eyes will open starting around ten days of age, and their ears around two weeks. This age marks the beginning of rapid mental and physical growth. They will attempt to walk at two weeks of age. Be sure to give them solid footing (*not* slippery newspaper!).

The dam will usually begin to wean her pups by four to six weeks of age;

smaller pups may need to stay with her longer. At around three weeks you can introduce the puppies to food: baby food or baby cereal or dry dog food mixed with water and put through the blender is a good starter. They may lick it off your finger or you may have to put their noses in it. No matter what technique you use, be prepared to declare the feeding arena a major disaster area by the time the meal is over. Puppies seem to think they can best eat with their feet!

A Good Home for Life

After about six weeks of age, it is important that the puppies meet people so that they are well socialized, but this does not mean that they need to be exposed to a constant stream of new faces. Young puppies are irresistible, and your house may become the newest tourist attraction on the block. Don't let the puppies be overhandled, and don't allow the mother to become stressed by onlookers. Talk to your veterinarian about your puppies' vaccination schedule and visitors, who could bring contagious diseases with them.

There are two ways to place puppies: the ethical way and the unethical way. The unethical way is easy: sell each pup to the first comer for whatever you can get, and as soon as it leaves your house wipe your hands of it. Don't think about the new owner who may not have a clue about raising a dog, who may think a Cavalier will be a fine outdoor watchdog, or who is simply desperate for a Christmas present for the kids but really has no desire to keep it past the time they tire of it, or who wants a little moneymaker that will be a puppy machine living in a cage until it dies of neglect. Yes, the unethical way is easy, until you try to sleep at night—every night for the next 12 years or so as you lie awake wondering what fate you sealed for the little being who trusted you to care about its future.

Getting into all that mischief is hard work—but somebody's got to do it!

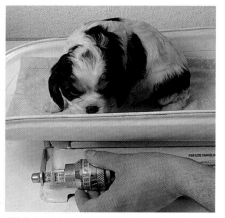

Weigh each puppy every day for the first two weeks.

The ethical way is initially more difficult, but will be easier if you have quality puppies with which to attract quality homes. If you have a quality breeding, word of mouth within the Cavalier world and at dog shows will be your best advertisement, but you can supplement with ads in dog magazines and in various newspapers. You must play detective in ascertaining if prospective buyers have the sort of home in which you would be comfortable placing a puppy. Once a sale has been made, the ethical breeder maintains contact with the puppy owner. Finally, the ethical breeder agrees that no matter what the age and what the reason, if the new owner can no longer keep the dog, it is always welcome back at its birthplace. If you can't make the commitment to be an ethical breeder, please don't be a breeder at all.

The Cavalier Competitor

Upon emerging from the obscurity of the miscellaneous class, most newly recognized AKC breeds mind their manners and only slowly gain a foothold as full-fledged competitors. Not the Cavalier. Since officially being welcomed into the toy group, the Cavalier has been downright pushy, hogging Best-in-Group awards and not being at all shy about claiming a few Best in Shows. Nor have they stopped there. Although they were already eligible to compete in obedience trials, their numbers seem to have swelled, and they continue to lay claim to their share of high-scoring toy awards. No babes in toyland, Cavaliers are proving themselves to be game for just about any challenge put before them.

Cavalcade of Cavaliers

The Cavalier leads the toy group around the group ring, and it appears to have let this placement go to its head. Although the success of Cavaliers in the show ring may seem instantaneous, it is only because showing is really nothing new for Cavaliers and their owners. Cavaliers and their Toy Spaniel ancestors have been a steady presence in the show rings of England since the turn of the century. In fact, it could be said that the Cavalier King Charles Spaniel was born at a dog show, since it was Roswell Eldridge's challenge in the form of a class prize offered at the Crufts show in 1926 that planted the seed for the breed. Crufts is one of the largest and most prestigious shows in the world, and so perhaps it was only fitting that in the 1973 show the fruits of that seed, in the form of Ch Alansmere Aquarius, was judged Best in Show at Crufts over thousands of dogs representing over a hundred other breeds. Perhaps one day soon Crufts' American counterpart, the Westminster Dog Show, will be conquered by another Englander.

Even in the United States, the Cavalier is no newcomer to dog shows. The CKCSC, USA has held its own shows and awarded its own championships for decades. With entries sometimes numbering in the hundreds, winning any award at these events is no small feat. The result of the importation of dogs from top English lines, combined with the tough competition among American dogs,

The show Cavalier must learn to pose on lead.

With their happy "look at me" attitude, Cavaliers are natural showdogs.

ther spayed nor neutered, or (if male) has two normally descended testicles, it can be shown, but if your Cav isn't really show quality most breeders would prefer you not to show it. It's sometimes hard to win with your first show prospect, but you will still learn a lot about the show world and be better prepared in case you would like to show your next Cavalier (of course you will have more than one!).

Once in the show ring the judge examines each Cavalier from head to tail and ranks each in accordance with its adherence to the official breed standard. The show dog must trot merrily about the ring and pose when stopped. It must be able to stand posed on a table without showing resentment or shyness when the judge examines it. This is seldom a problem for most Cavaliers, of course; the challenge is to keep them from jumping into the judge's arms!

There are professional handlers who will show your dog for you and probably win more often than you would; however, there is nothing like the thrill of winning when you are on the other end of the lead!

Because Cavaliers are so much a true family member, it can hurt to have your beloved dog placed last in its class. Just be sure that your Cav doesn't catch on and always treat your dog like a Best in Show winner whether its gets a blue ribbon or no ribbon at all. To survive as a conformation competitor you must be able to separate your own ego and self-esteem from your dog. You must also not allow your dog's ability to win in the ring cloud your perception of your dog's true worth in its primary role: that of friend and companion.

has resulted in a breed that is poised to compete at the highest caliber of competition. If you have visions of competing with your Cavalier in conformation events, be forewarned that you are going to need a good one.

Don't be surprised if it takes you a year or more to find a good show Cavalier; part of this time will be spent learning the standard, studying the breed, and talking with breeders. The Royal Spaniels magazine is an essential aid in your quest. It's best to get your show Cavalier from a successful breeder, preferably one located fairly close to you. This way the breeder can help show you how to groom and prepare your dog for the ring, and give you tips on showing it.

The breeder should also be able to give you an honest opinion about your Cav's good and bad points, and its chances of success in the ring. As long as your Cavalier is at least six months of age, AKC registered, is nei-

Mind Games

If your Cavalier is more than just another pretty face, you may wish to enter an obedience trial, where your little gifted one can earn degrees attesting to its mastery of various levels of obedience. You and your Cav will have to prove yourselves in front of a judge at three different obedience trials in order to officially have an obedience title become part of your dog's name.

You plan on training your Cavalier the commands Heel, Sit, Down, Come, and Stay for use in everyday life. Add the Stand for Exam, and your dog will have the basic skills necessary to earn the AKC Companion Dog (CD) title. The AKC will send you a free pamphlet describing obedience trial regulations.

The AKC CD title requires the dog to do the following:

1. Heel on-lead, sitting automatically each time you stop, negotiating right, left, and about-turns without guidance from you, and changing to a faster and slower pace

2. Heel in a figure 8 around two people, still on-lead

3. Stand still off-lead six feet away from you and allow a judge to touch it

4. Do the exercises in number 1, except off-lead

5. Come to you when called from 20 feet away, and then return to heel position on command

6. Stay in a sitting position with a group of other dogs, while you are 20 feet away, for one minute

7. Stay in a down position with the same group while you are 20 feet away, for three minutes

Higher degrees of Companion Dog Excellent (CDX), Utility Dog (UD), Utility Dog Excellent (UDX), and Obedience Trial Champion (OTCH) also may require retrieving, jumping, hand signals and scent discrimination.

If you enter competition with your Cavalier, remember this as your Golden Rule: Companion Dog means just that; being upset at your dog because it messed up defeats the pur-

Agility combines running, jumping, and obedience, and is loads of fun for people and dogs.

pose of obedience as a way of promoting a harmonious partnership between trainer and dog. Failing a trial, in the scope of life, is an insignificant event. Never let a ribbon or a few points become more important than a trusting relationship with your companion. Remember, your Cavalier will forgive you for the times you mess up!

Hot on the Trail

Most people don't consider a toy breed a likely candidate for a tracking dog, but most toy breeds aren't the hardy Cavalier. With its outdoor heritage, the Cavalier will welcome the opportunity to get its feet dirty and breathe in the great outdoors. Many will also embrace the challenge of following a scent trail.

Some dogs have a more innate tendency to trail, but all breeds can be taught to use their noses and track. A Tracking Dog (TD) title is earned by following a human trail about

If you can dream it, you and your Cavalier can do it. Still, it takes a special team of owner and dog to earn the titles that "Picadilly" (Maxholt Special Love Story), the most titled Cavalier in history, has achieved: CKCSC/CAN/BDA/SKC/CDA Champion: U-UD Maxholt Special Love Story, AKC UDX, CAN/BDA OTCH SKC UD: CDA CD, TT, CGC.

500 yards long that was laid up to two hours earlier. More advanced titles of Tracking Dog Excellent (TDX) and Variable Surface Tracker (VST) can also be earned.

King of the Hill

Competitive agility was accepted as an AKC competition around the same time that Cavaliers were accepted as an AKC breed. Both have taken the dog world by storm. Dogs fly through a course of obstacles that may include a tunnel, narrow bridge, seesaw, jumps, and a pause on command. Classes are divided by height, and there are Novice, Open, and Excellent divisions. The AKC confers, in increasing level of difficulty, the titles Novice Agility Dog (NAD), Open Agility Dog (OAD), Agility Dog Excellent (ADE), and Master Agility Excellent (MAX).

Cavaliers are one of the most versatile of the toy breeds when it comes to competing successfully in a variety of fields. Despite this, most Cavaliers never step foot into a ring, and never win a ribbon. They don't have to. They've already won the biggest prize of all—their owner's hearts.

The Cavalier Companion

Cavaliers and their owners tend to share an almost uncanny bond, as well as an eagerness to share all aspects of their lives. Although snuggling in front of the hearth may be sufficient for some people and their dogs, others will want to include their dogs on greater adventures.

The Gypsy King

Whether you are journeying around the country or around the block, you and your Cavalier will be held up to scrutiny by people who have seen too many ill-mannered dogs. For the sake of dog ownership in the future, maintain the highest public standards:
• Always clean up after your dog. Carry a little plastic bag for disposal later.
• Don't let your dog run loose where it could bother picnickers, bicyclists, joggers, or children.
• Never let your dog bark unchecked.
• Never let your dog jump up on people.
• Never take a chance of your dog's biting anybody.

Cavaliers make excellent travel companions. They are small enough to fit handily into any car, yet large enough to share most outdoor adventures along the way. A dog gives you a good excuse to stop and enjoy the scenery up close, and maybe even get some exercise along the way. With proper planning, you will find that a Cavalier companion can make your trip even better.

Without proper planning, sharing your trip with any dog can be a nightmare, as you are turned away from motels, parks, and beaches. It's no fun sleeping in your car, or trying to sneak a dog past the front desk of a motel. Several books are available listing establishments that accept pets. Call ahead to attractions to see if they have arrangements for pets.

Whether you will be spending your nights at a motel, campground, or even a friend's home, always have your dog on its very best behavior. Ask beforehand if it will be OK for you to bring your Cavalier. Have your dog clean and parasite-free. Do not allow your dog to run helter-skelter through the homes of friends. Bring your dog's own clean blanket or bed, or better yet, its cage. Your Cav will appreciate

The well-mannered Cavalier is a welcome visitor.

The Cavalier seatbelt: its cage firmly strapped in the backseat of the car.

Always walk your Cavalier on lead when away from home. If frightened or distracted, your dog could become disoriented and lost. The long retractable leads are excellent for traveling. Keep an eye out for little nature excursions, which are wonderful for refreshing both dog and owner. But always do so with a cautious eye; never risk your own or your dog's safety by stopping in totally desolate locales, no matter how breathtaking the view.

While in the car your Cavalier will want to cuddle in your lap or close by your side, or hang its head out the window for a big whiff of country air. You are smarter than your Cavalier, however, and know that it should always ride with the equivalent of a doggy seat belt: the cage. Not only can a cage help prevent accidents by keeping your dog from using your lap as a trampoline, but if an accident does happen a cage can save your dog's life. A cage with a padlocked door can also be useful when you need to leave the dog in the car with the windows down.

Although car trips are the most common mode of travel for dogs, sometimes an airplane trip is required (note that dogs are not allowed on trains). Small dogs are often able to ride in the passenger cabin of an airplane, if their cage can fit under the seat. Always opt for this choice if available. Ask when making reservations what type of cage you must have. If you must ship a dog by itself, it is better to ship "counter to counter" than to ship as air freight. Don't feed your dog before traveling. The cage should have a small dish that can be attached to the door. The night before the trip fill it with water and freeze it; as it melts during the flight the dog will have water that otherwise would have spilled out during the loading process. Also include a large chewbone to occupy your jet-setter. Be

the familiar place to sleep, and your friends and motel owners will breathe sighs of relief. Even though your dog may be accustomed to sleeping on furniture at home, a proper canine guest stays on the floor when visiting.

Walk and walk your dog (and clean up after it) to make sure no accidents occur inside. If they do, clean them immediately. Don't leave any surprises for your hosts! Changes in water or food, or simply stress can often result in diarrhea, so be particularly attentive to taking your dog out often.

Never, never leave your dog unattended in a strange place. The dog's perception is that you have left and forgotten it; it either barks or tries to dig its way out through the doors and windows in an effort to find you, or becomes upset and relieves itself on the carpet. Always remember that anyone who allows your dog to spend the night is doing so with a certain amount of trepidation; make sure your Cavalier is so well behaved that they invite both of you back.

sure to line the cage with soft, absorbent material, preferably something that can be thrown away if soiled. Although air compartments are heated, they are not air-conditioned, and in hot weather dogs have been known to overheat while the plane was still on the runway. Never ship in the heat of day.

Items for your Cavalier's own travel case:
• first aid kit
• heartworm preventive and any other medications, especially antidiarrhea medication
• food and water bowls
• dog biscuits and chewies
• flea spray
• flea comb and brush
• bedding
• short and long leashes
• sweater for cold weather
• flashlight for night walks
• plastic baggies or other poop disposal means
• moist towelettes, paper towels, and self-rinse shampoo
• food
• bottled water or water from home— many dogs are very sensitive to changes in water and can develop diarrhea
• license tags, including a tag indicating where you could be reached while on your trip, or including the address of someone you know will be at home
• health and rabies certificates
• recent color photo in case your Cav somehow gets lost

With a little foresight you may find your Cavalier King Charles Spaniel to be the most entertaining and enjoyable travel companion you could invite along. And don't be surprised if you find your dog nestled in your suitcase among your packed clothes!

Boarding

Sometimes you must leave your dog behind when you travel. Ask friends or your veterinarian for boarding kennel recommendations. The ideal kennel will be approved by the American Boarding Kennel Association, have climate-controlled accommodations, and will keep your Cavalier either indoors or in a combination indoor/outdoor run. Make an unannounced visit to the kennel and ask to see the facilities. While you can't expect spotlessness and a perfumed atmosphere, most runs should be clean and the odor should not be overpowering. All dogs should have clean water and at least some dogs should have soft bedding. Good kennels will require proof of immunizations, and an incoming check for fleas. They will allow you to bring toys and bedding, and will administer prescribed medication. Strange dogs should not be allowed to mingle, and the entire kennel area should be fenced.

Your dog may be more comfortable if an experienced pet sitter or responsible friend comes to your home and feeds and exercises your dog regularly. This works best if you have a doggy door. The kid next door is seldom a good choice for this important responsibility. It is too easy for the dog to slip out the door, or for signs of illness to go unnoticed, unless the sitter is an experienced dog person. The life of your dog is a heavy responsibility for a child. A bonded pet sitter may cost a little more, but is well worth the extra peace of mind.

Whatever means you choose, always leave emergency numbers and your veterinarian's name. Make arrangements with your veterinarian to treat your dog for any problems that may arise. This means leaving a written agreement stating that you give permission for treatment and accept responsibility for charges.

Take a Hike!

Cavaliers can entertain themselves quite ably within the confines of your own yard, but they will jump at the

In unfamiliar territory, always walk your Cavalier on leash.

chance for an adventure afield. Regular exercise is the cure for many behavioral problems, especially in younger dogs.

Cavaliers make wonderful short-distance hiking companions, but their Spaniel heritage will sometimes lead them astray unless you keep an eye on them. Bringing along another reliable dog that stays with you is the best training aid you can have.

Know your running area thoroughly before ever removing your Cav's leash. Is there a road around the bend in a path? A fast-running canal? A cliff? Alligators? Porcupines? Mine shafts? Caves? Burrows? Thin ice? Explore an area with your dog on a long lead several times before trusting it off-lead. Practice your "Come" command in a fenced ball field and make sure your Cavalier is returning reliably before trusting it in the wide open spaces.

Everybody thinks their dog is smart and trustworthy and reliable off-lead. They are usually right—until the unpredictable occurs: another dog attacks, or a cat runs underfoot. Whatever the reason, the trustworthy dog forgets itself for just a moment—and that's all it takes to run in front of a car. Trust is wonderful, but careless or blind trust is deadly.

In many areas there simply are no safe places in which to run your Cavalier off-lead. Your dog can get ample exercise and enjoyment from a walk on-lead. Before walking on-lead double check that your dog's collar cannot slip over its head. A startled dog can frantically back out of its collar unless it is snug. If you use a retractable leash, never allow so much loose lead that your dog could suddenly jump into the path of a passing vehicle.

Check your dog's foot pads regularly for signs of abrasion, foreign bodies, tears, or blistering from hot pavement. Leave your dog at home in hot weather. Dogs are unable to cool themselves through sweating, and heatstroke in jogging dogs is a common emergency seen by veterinarians in the summer. In winter, check between the foot pads for balls of ice (clipping the long hair between the pads and coating the paws with Vaseline can help keep the ice balls down somewhat) and rinse the feet when returning from walking on rock salt. If you pick a regular time of day for your walk you will have your own personal fitness coach goading you off the couch like clockwork.

Swimming is an excellent exercise, especially in the summer or for dogs with arthritis or other injuries. Most Cavaliers take right to the water, but if you have one that needs a little coaxing, get right into the water with it and ease it gradually in. Support its rear end so that it doesn't splash on top of the water, and you will soon have a little otter on your hands.

Little Dog Lost

Cavaliers have a tendency to go where the wind blows them. When they quit sniffing flowers and chasing butterflies, they look up and suddenly realize they don't know where they are. Of course you must never allow your Cav to find itself in such a situation, but if your dog does wander off, you need to act quickly. Don't rely on the dog's fabled ability to find its way home. You only hear about the few who make it. Too many dogs seem to have no sense of direction.

Start your search at the very worst place you could imagine your dog going, usually the nearest highway. Don't drive recklessly and endanger your own dog's life should it run across the road. If you still can't find your pet, get pictures of

Puppies should be introduced to the great outdoors in only the very safest of areas.

your dog and go door to door; ask any workers or delivery persons in the area. Call the local animal control, police department, and veterinarians. If your dog is tattooed or microchipped, contact the registry. Make up large posters with a picture of your dog or a similar looking Cavalier. Take out an ad in the local paper. Mention a reward, but do not specify an amount.

As Cavaliers continue to gain public attention they will become increasingly attractive to dognappers. Never leave your dog in a place where it could be taken. Never give anyone reward money before seeing your dog. There are a number of scams involving answering lost dog ads, many asking for money for shipping the dog back to you from a distance or for paying vet bills, when very often these people have not really found your dog. If your

97

dog is tattooed, you can have the person read the tattoo to you in order to positively identify it.

Even license tags cannot always ensure your dog's return, because they must be on the dog to be effective. Tattooing your social security number or your dog's registration number on the inside of its thigh provides a permanent means of identification; these numbers can be registered with one of the several lost pet recovery agencies. Microchips are available that are placed under the dog's skin with a simple injection. They contain information about the dog and cannot be removed, but require a special scanner (owned by most animal shelters) to be read. You may wish to discuss this option with your veterinarian or local breeders.

The Comforter Spaniel

Cavaliers excel at many roles, but it is no surprise that their forte is the role of companion par excellence. The

The Cavalier is still fulfilling its role as a comforter spaniel par excellence!

Cavalier's first claim to fame was as a "comforter spaniel," bred to bring both physical and emotional comfort to those whose lives it graced. Today the role of the comforter spaniel is as vital as ever.

As more of the population becomes elderly and either unable to care for or keep a pet, the result is particularly sad for lonely people who may have relied upon the comfort and companionship of a pet throughout most of their independent years. Studies have shown that pet ownership increases life expectancy and petting animals can lower blood pressure. In recent years nursing home residents have come to look forward to visits by dogs, including today's comforter spaniel, the Cavalier. These dogs must be meticulously well-mannered and well-groomed; to be registered as a Certified Therapy Dog a dog must demonstrate that it will act in an obedient, outgoing, gentle manner to strangers. The loving Cavalier is still comforting after all these years.

Pledge of Allegiance

You have a lifetime of experiences to share with your Cavalier King Charles Spaniel. The remainder of your dog's life will be spent under your care and guidance. Your life may change dramatically in the years to come: marriage, divorce, new baby, new home—for better or worse, your dog will still depend on you and still love you. Always remember the promise you made to yourself and your future puppy before you made the commitment to share your life: to keep your interest in your dog and care for it everyday of its life with as much love and enthusiasm as you did the first day it arrived home.

Useful Addresses and Literature

Organizations
American Kennel Club, Inc.
51 Madison Avenue
New York, NY 10038
212-696-8200

AKC Registration
5580 Centerview Drive
Suite 200
Raleigh, NC 27606-3390
919-233-9767

Cavalier King Charles Spaniel
  Club, USA
Jan Wendell
1130 E. Linden St.
Rockport, TX 78382-3011
512-729-5648
(address changes periodically)

CKCSC, USA Rescue
Linda Kornhi
541-726-3850
(address changes periodically)

American Cavalier King Charles
  Spaniel Club, Inc.
Martha Guimond
1905 Upper Ridge Rd.
Greenlake, PA 18054
(address changes periodically)

ACKCS Rescue
Cathy Gish
657 Glenwood Dr.
Henderson, KY 42420-2105
(address changes periodically)

The Cavalier King Charles
  Spaniel Club
Mrs. Leslie Jupp
60 Roundway
Copped Hall, Camberly, Surrey
Great Britain
(address changes periodically)

Orthopedic Foundation for
  Animals
2300 Nifong Blvd.
Columbia, MO 65201
314-442-0418

Home Again Microchip Service
1-800-LONELY-ONE

Books
Booth, Evelyn. All About
  Cavalier King Charles
  Spaniels. England: Pelham
  Books, 1983.
Burgess, Susan. The Cavalier
  King Charles Spaniel.
  England: Dog Owner's
  Library, 1975.
Smith, Sheila. Cavalier King
  Charles Spaniels Today. New
  York: Howell Book House,
  1995.

Periodicals
Dog Fancy
P.O. Box 53264
Boulder, CO 80322-3264
303-666-8504

Dogs USA Annual
P.O. Box 55811
Boulder, CO 80322-5811
303-786-7652

Dog World
29 North Wacker Dr.
Chicago, IL 60606-3298
312-726-2802

Top Notch Toys
8848 Beverly Hills
Lakeland, FL 33809-1604
941-858-3839

The Royal Spaniels
14531 Jefferson St.
Midway City, CA 92655
714-893-0053

Your Cavalier will be your partner and soulmate for the rest of its life—and it expects no less from you.

Index

A Ruby in the rough, all Cavalier King Charles Spaniels are precious gems.